GLASGOW'S GREATEST HITS

GLASGOW'S GREATEST HITS

TALES FROM THE CITY OF MUSIC

**FIONA SHEPHERD,
ALISON STROAK & JONATHAN TREW**

Polygon

First published in Great Britain in 2025 by Polygon,
an imprint of Birlinn Ltd.

Birlinn Ltd
West Newington House
10 Newington Road
Edinburgh
EH9 1QS

www.polygonbooks.co.uk

1

ISBN 978 1 84697 706 0
eBook ISBN 978 1 78885 779 6

British Library Cataloguing-in-Publication Data
A catalogue record for this book is available on request
from the British Library.

Design by Alison Rae
Typesetting by 3btype, Edinburgh

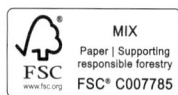

MIX
Paper | Supporting
responsible forestry
FSC® C007785

Printed and bound by Bell & Bain Ltd, Glasgow.

CONTENTS

For Glaswegians, Glasgow is the centre of the universe and we intend to reflect that.

> – broadcaster Tony Currie recalling Radio Clyde's original mission statement

3·00

49

REGULAR MUSIC LTD.
proudly presents

CLYDE 2
1152 AM

DAVID BOWIE

plus special guest DJ PATHAAN
at **BARROWLAND, GLASGOW**
on **TUESDAY, 22nd JULY, 1997**
Doors open 7.00 p.m.

Ticket £15.00
ing fee)

№ 0325

RVES THE RIGHT OF ADMISSION

JESUS and MARY CHA

at BARROWLAND, GLASGOW
IDAY, 11th SEPTEMBER, 19

£5.00
nce
en at 7.30 p.m.

t reserve the right of

CONCERT
REGULAR MUSIC
ESTIVALS LTD.
LOCK X
£10.00

DANCE FACTORY PRESENTS
presents

The Damned

plus support
at
GLASGOW BARROWLANDS
on
SATURDAY, 18th OCTOBER, 1986
DOORS 7-00 p.m.
£5-00 ADVANCE

№ 001651

GLASG

MAY 8

PCL Pre

the White
& the Von F

een Marga
University Avenu
ursday 15th No
£9.00 (Subject To
Doors 7:3

non students, no signingi
perate licensed bar availa
Proof of

Regular Music
presents

PUBLIC ENEMY

with guests

at **GLASGOW BARROWLAND**
WEDNESDAY, 12th JULY, 1995
open at 7.00 p.m.
et £13.50 **A** № 0142
ing fee)

ncerts

ans

HOUSE of PAIN

PLUS SPECIAL GUESTS
CYPRESS HILL
FunkDoobiest
OWLAND BALLROOM GLASGOW
ednesday 14th July 1993
ckets £10.00 In Advance
(Subject to booking fee)
DOORS OPEN 7:00 p.m.

CTIONS, OVER 18'S ONLY MAY BE
OF OF AGE MAY BE ASKED FOR
D.

REGULAR MUSIC
present

THE
TONE ROSES

Saturday 9th June
in
**THE BIG TOP
GLASGOW GREEN**

Tickets
£14.00
(plus booking fee)

ates Open 6.30 pm
On Stage 10.00 pm

№ 2560

REGULAR MUSIC
present

№

THE
STONE
ROSES

SATURDAY 9TH JUNE 1990
in **THE BIG TOP**,
GLASGOW GREEN
(see local press for exact location)

GATES OPEN 6.30 PM, BAND ON STAGE 10.00

Regular Music Ltd.
presents

mogwai

with special guests
at **BARROWLAND, GLASGOW**
on **SATURDAY, 23rd OCTOBER,**
Doors open 7.00 p.m.

Ticket £8.50
plus booking fee
№ 1614

MANAGEMENT RESERVES THE RIGHT OF ADMISSION.
OVER 18'S ONLY. I.D. MAY BE REQUIRED.
THIS TICKET CANNOT BE EXCHANGED OR REFUNDED.

Coach Travel Hotline: 0131 226 6

LAR MUSIC
presents

AMONES

s Guests

WLAND GLASGOW
2nd OCTOBER, 1989

p.m.

№ 436

BELLE AND
SEBASTIAN

REGULAR MUSIC

presents

JEFF BUCKLEY

with guests

REG

TH

at BAR
on FRIDA

Doors open at
Advance Tic

PREFACE

When Glasgow was awarded UNESCO City of Music status in 2008, it was lauded for 'the vibrancy of its music scene and its role as a world player in music'. Seventeen years later, as the city celebrates its 850th birthday, it can still comfortably claim to be Scotland's music capital.

Glasgow is home to such august arts institutions as Scottish Opera, the Royal Conservatoire of Scotland and the Royal Scottish National Orchestra. It is also a voracious festival city, and TRNSMT, Celtic Connections, Glasgow Jazz Festival and Piping Live, among many others, feed that appetite. But the city's musical reputation is truly founded on its dynamic grassroots network of small venues, independent record labels, studios and the endlessly creative artists and bands who populate them year-round.

Glasgow Music City Tours was founded to applaud that scene, extol our heritage and, in particular, to share the weird, wild and wonderful stories which have sprung from this most entertaining of histories. The riotous anecdotes we have unearthed and also gleaned from our guests over the years have only confirmed that nowhere does patter better than Glasgow.

Glasgow's Greatest Hits collects our most beloved stories and celebrates our favourite musicians, venues and concerts from across the decades, even centuries. It is by no means comprehensive, nor is it unbiased, but we hope it captures the spirit of the city's music scene in all its gallus glory.

FOREWORD

'What is it about Glasgow?' they ask. 'Is it in the water?'

The cliché has always irritated me, it feels shallow and patronising. But sometimes, listening to evening music radio, I'll hear a song I *know* has been written and performed by a band from (or around) Glasgow. I find it difficult to define. Techno or pop, indie or rock, I can hear an ineffable melancholy, a lilt or a kink that can only be a product of my beloved, forlorn, glamorously wrecked city. Hard men, hardened women laughing it all away.

It's in the disappointed romanticism of The Blue Nile, the busy ironic dandyism of early Orange Juice, the ambitious modernism of Simple Minds and the melodious punk of Teenage Fanclub. It's in the vivacious sadness of Camera Obscura, the harmonic distortion of Mogwai, the sentimental joy of Altered Images. It infects the kernel of work by artists and musicians who have adopted Glasgow as their base in their student days (David Shrigley, Franz Ferdinand and Lloyd Cole come to mind).

It's not in the water we drink but in the reflections found in all that water in the streets. In puddles and gutters, our post-industrial town throws the heavens and Hollywood back up to us as we spend our nights looking down, cringing in the inevitable rain, on our way to a show where callow types will synthesise The Byrds and The Staple Singers or Iggy Pop and Nina Simone. It's in our universal love for The Velvet Underground – street savvy, sardonic and hopelessly in pursuit of love and emancipation.

It's a dirty secret. But to look down and see beyond, with optimism and belief, means we have a soul unlimited by the depredations the powers that be have inflicted on our city and its exceptional buildings, its world-class working-class sensibility. Those gap sites, no man's lands and roads to nowhere shine with the standing water that holds our hopes and dreams.

Justin Currie

The sensational Alex Harvey pictured on the Clutha mural.

FOUNDING FATHERS

ALEX HARVEY

While his musical career spanned almost three decades and genres ranging from skiffle to R&B via soul and pop, it was as the theatrical frontman of glam rock outfit the Sensational Alex Harvey Band, aka SAHB, that our Kinning Park-born hero will be remembered. Alexander James Harvey first achieved a national profile in 1957 when he won a talent competition to find 'Scotland's Tommy Steele'. A striking sobriquet but not one that led to immediate riches – the youthful Alex and his band resorted to stealing spuds from farmers' fields to feed themselves on the subsequent tour.

Other pre-SAHB adventures included a stint in the pit band for the hippie musical *Hair* and the release of his 1964 album *Alex Harvey And His Soul Band*, a recording which many hail as Scotland's first ever rock album.

Formed in 1972 with members of the band Tear Gas, the SAHB would go on to be the biggest noise in Scottish rock for much of the 70s. Songs such as 'The Boston Tea Party' and 'Delilah' made a splash in the charts, while their dramatic live shows are still recalled fondly by music lovers of a certain vintage (see Apollo gigs entry on page 75).

Alex died prematurely of a heart attack in 1982 but he inspired a generation of Scottish rockers. Not least AC/DC's Bon Scott. With his mischievous grin and trademark black-and-white hooped jumper, Alex was a larger-than-life character on and off stage. Less well known was his obsession with a certain water-based Highland myth. A fascination that led to the K-Tel album *Alex Harvey Presents The Loch Ness Monster*. This 1977, mainly spoken-word album, now deleted, is even more rarely spotted than its eponymous cryptid.

Marie McDonald McLaughlin Lawrie: a mouthful of a name, 'a lulu of a kid'.

LULU

Weeeeeeeellllllll, where to begin with Lulu? This true Glasgow icon has a CV like no other, from Eurovision Song Contest winner to Bond theme diva to primetime TV host and sometime actor.

The Dennistoun lass, born Marie McDonald McLaughlin Lawrie, was discovered singing at the Lindella Club in the city centre in 1962 and hailed as 'a lulu of a kid' by her manager Marion Massey. This pocket rocket broke the microphone with the unfettered power of her voice while recording her debut single 'Shout', an Isley Brothers number she first heard performed by local hero Alex Harvey. She went on to score hits with songs by David Bowie and Neil Diamond, as well as the *Ulysses*-quoting 'Love Loves to Love Love', and she also topped the US charts with 'To Sir With Love'. Jimmy Page played on Lulu's debut album *Something To Shout About* and she cemented Glasgow's love affair with southern soul by recording her 1970 *New Routes* album in Alabama's newly founded Muscle Shoals Sound Studio – a reminder of the credibility she was accorded as an R&B singer.

At the same time, Lulu was a mainstream TV fixture, hosting a succession of variety shows with guests as diverse as Aretha Franklin,

Dudley Moore, Sergio Mendes and, most notoriously, Jimi Hendrix, who was banned by the BBC after changing songs mid-stream and overshooting the transmission time on *Happening For Lulu*.

Her later career was a patchwork affair but she returned in the early 90s to score a UK number one guesting with Take That on 'Relight My Fire' and wrote the 1993 Tina Turner hit 'I Don't Wanna Fight', which was inspired by her own marriage to Bee Gee Maurice Gibb. She appeared as herself on *Absolutely Fabulous*, later taking the line 'Champagne for Lulu!' as the name of her 2024 retirement tour, which marked her sixtieth year in showbusiness.

JOHN MARTYN

He may have been born Iain David McGeachy in Surrey, but the man who would become John Martyn was made in Glasgow after his family moved to Tantallon Road in Shawlands. This singular singer, songwriter and guitarist cut his musical teeth in the city's folk clubs, where his confidence and charisma did not go unnoticed by peers such as Billy Connolly, Rab Noakes and Linda Thompson. Mentored – or should that be aided and abetted – by Hamish Imlach (see page 10), another musician with an appetite for wild times, Martyn's talent was such that he seamlessly straddled folk, jazz, rock and blues in a career which spanned more than forty years.

For many, his finest album is 1973's *Solid Air*, a work which featured contributions from Pentangle bassist Danny Thompson. The pair had an affinity for mayhem as much as music. Curiously, carpets featured regularly in their debauches.

We like the story of Thompson nailing a passed-out Martyn to the floor under a hotel room carpet. The next morning, Thompson ordered a room-service breakfast which he consumed with great gusto in front of his increasingly apoplectic, thirsty and hungover compadre.

FRANKIE MILLER

Born in Bridgeton in 1949, Francis John Miller could deftly turn his hand to R&B, rock and soul, but the one constant was his powerfully gravelly voice, the grit in his musical oyster. In the 70s and 80s, Miller put this to good effect covering songs such as 'Be Good To Yourself' and 'Darlin'', while his 1991 version of Dougie MacLean's 'Caledonia' provoked lumps in many a throat when it was used in a Tennent's Lager ad.

Indeed, Rod Stewart reckoned that Frankie was the only white singer to have brought a tear to his eye. Perhaps he asked Rod to get a round in. When not making Rod cry, Frankie was highly successful as a songwriter with his work covered by acts as diverse as the Eagles, Bob Seger, Bonnie Tyler, Joe Cocker and Ray Charles. Not content with being musically gifted, Frankie showed great promise as an actor – most notably as hardman Jake McQuillan in Peter McDougall's 1979 Play for Today *Just a Boy's Game.*

Tragedy struck in 1994 when Frankie suffered a brain haemorrhage in New York and subsequent years have been spent in rehabilitation. Frankie's creative spark was not silenced. His 2016 album *Frankie Miller's Double Take* featured old recordings of the singer remastered into duets with artists including Elton John, Willie Nelson and, more incongruously, Kid Rock.

And, while we are dropping names, Sir Billy Connolly is an old Glasgow pal of Frankie's. He swears that his friend had unconventional rock star habits. In particular, he would always have an electric frying pan with him when touring so he could cook up some mince 'n' tatties for a wee taste of home.

SIMPLE MINDS

Simple Minds are Glasgow to the core, but from their earliest days there was something aspirational about the group. Maybe it was the tower-block upbringing of Toryglen boys Jim Kerr and Charlie Burchill, eyes on the horizon, dreaming of Europe.

The Minds went on to conquer the stadia of Europe and beyond, but if you squint the right way it is not that difficult to reconcile the composers of big-ticket anthems 'Mandela Day' and 'Belfast Child' with the southside weirdos in eyeliner who emerged from the ashes of local punk band Johnny & the Self-Abusers.

The Self-Abusers split on the day of their only single release, 'Saints and Sinners'. At one of their last gigs, in scuzzy St Enoch Square club Terminal 1, the DJ played Donna Summer's 'I Feel Love'. It was an epiphany moment for Kerr, who declared to his bandmates, 'We need to get a synth – punk's finished.'

Casting off their punk monikers – Kerr was known as Pripton Weird and Burchill as Charlie Argue – they formed Simple Minds and played their first gig in January 1978 at the Apollo's nightclub, Satellite City,

Simple Minds' frontman Jim Kerr moves on up to the waterfront.

supporting reggae legends Steel Pulse (also on the bill were a bunch of young bucks called the Nu-Sonics, who would shortly change their name to Orange Juice). 'We walked on to silence, but walked off to mayhem,' Kerr recalled.

Simple Minds dreamed of making it out of the city, but Glasgow never left them. Over the years, they have celebrated their home-town in song, most famously on 'Waterfront', a titanic paean to the city's industrial history, heralded by Derek Forbes' behemoth of a bassline.

'Broken Glass Park', from their 2014 album *Big Music*, sprang from Kerr's memories of hanging around Queen's Park and harks back to the days of punk penury when the band members would share one drink, dubbed 'the people's pint', in Shawlands' Doune Castle pub, while the early classic 'Theme For Great Cities' was inspired not by Paris or Prague but by Priesthill and the sound of the ice-cream van trundling round his mum's neighbourhood. Its working title was 'Do You Want Anything From The Van?'

POSTCARD RECORDS

Glasgow came late to the independent record labels party – we can blame the council's ban on punk to some degree (see page 102) – but when the city did discover the joys of DIY music mogul-ing, it did so in style, with Postcard Records leading the charge.

Glasgow's first indie label of note and by far its most significant was founded by the Andy Warhol-loving Alan Horne and his musician pal Edwyn Collins, and it was run from the sock drawer of Horne's wardrobe in Flat 2/R, 185 West Princes Street.

They may have been limited of resources but they were lofty on aesthetic, aping Motown's strapline the Sound of Young America to hail their label as the Sound of Young Scotland. Postcard Records was brazenly pretentious and arrogant at a time when punk egalitarianism still ruled, with Horne in particular hailed by *NME* scribe Paul Morley as 'refreshingly spiteful and unimpressed'.

According to Malcolm Fisher of the Postcard-adjacent French Impressionists, every band on the label had to pass the Velvet Underground litmus test – with 60 per cent VU DNA considered the pass rate. Edwyn's band **Orange Juice** more than made the grade. Long before Franz Ferdinand, these guys were the new Scottish gentry, kitted out in charity shop buckskin jackets, paisley-patterned scarves

The DIY delights of Postcard Records: homemade artwork ranged from subverting Scotland's shortbread tin tartanalia to hand-colouring record sleeves. It looks like this particular Scottish Colourist went for the naive pop art approach.

and plaid shirts, with their musical ears trained on US west coast psychedelia and NY disco at least as much as on their post-punk peers.

Joining Edinburgh's Josef K and Australia's Go-Betweens on a selective roster was East Kilbride's **Aztec Camera**, led by teen guitar hero Roddy Frame. Along with Orange Juice, Frame was soon London – and chart – bound. Having immortalised his local pub, the Diplomat, on *High Land, Hard Rain* track 'Down the Dip', he wistfully commemorated the overnight ride from Glasgow's bus station on the ravishing song 'Killermont Street'.

Horne, meanwhile, folded Postcard after eighteen months, then set up the major-affiliated Swamplands with a similar lifespan and finally released Orange Juice's *Ostrich Churchyard* album on a revived Postcard in 1992, with a John Peel Session included in the track listing. With typical perversity, his latest record label action was the 2020 release of cult troubadour Paul Quinn's *Unadulterated/Unincorporated* box set in an eye-wateringly limited edition of three hundred copies.

LONNIE DONEGAN

Rock 'n' roll as we know it was born in Glasgow on 29 April 1931, in Bridgeton no less. Forgive the hyperbole, but this was the date and place of birth of one Anthony James Donegan, later known to the beat-crazy kids of the UK as Lonnie Donegan.

Donegan was one of the key emissaries of post-war popular music, an unlikely looking conduit for a raw new DIY music craze called skiffle, which fused elements of country, folk, blues and Dixieland jazz, turned up the tempo and blasted off down the line. No wonder most of the songs were about trains. Crucially, anyone could play skiffle. All you needed was a cheap acoustic guitar, a washboard and a tea-chest bass. It was punk before punk and Donegan was the King of Skiffle.

His breakneck cover of Leadbelly's 'Rock Island Line' was a hit on both sides of the Atlantic and there were twenty-five more of them to come through the late 50s, before he was superseded by the very artists he inspired, not least a Liverpudlian teen outfit called the Quarrymen. But to Paul McCartney, Lonnie Donegan will always be simply 'the man'.

MATT McGINN

Matt McGinn had lived a life – two years in an approved school, shop steward in various shipyards and a range of teaching posts – before he started writing comic poems and folk songs, rendered in a voice characterised as 'a mixture of lumpy porridge and broken glass'.

Self-styled as McGinn of the Calton, his East End upbringing on Ross Street, right by the Barras market, provided an endless supply of earthy material for pithy portraits such as 'The Two Heided Man' and 'The Gallowgate Calypso' but even McGinn was surprised to win a writing competition with his first attempt, 'The Foreman O'Rourke', and to find a fan in US folk legend Pete Seeger.

In October 1962, Seeger arranged for him to perform at New York's prestigious Carnegie Hall, where McGinn was introduced to a young folk singer, Robert Zimmerman. The soon-to-be Bob Dylan played him a song he had written the previous day, 'A Hard Rain's A-Gonna Fall', and asked his advice on how to break through in Britain. Dylan was paid $60 for the gig; McGinn commanded a $200 fee. 'Me, I start at the top,' he quipped. 'From then on, it had to be down all the way.'

McGinn died aged forty-eight from smoke inhalation. Some of his ashes were scattered on the grave of the great socialist activist

Glasgow folk legends Matt McGinn and Hamish Imlach share a laugh on the Clutha mural.

John Maclean. Despite his commitment to left-wing politics, McGinn had acquired a reputation as a man who quit the Communist Party so frequently that Glasgow HQ were thinking of issuing a book of perforated cards for him to tear up at will.

HAMISH IMLACH

Like Matt McGinn, Hamish Imlach was a huge figure on Glasgow's folk revival scene of the 60s and 70s – in more ways than one. This rotund raconteur was born in Calcutta to Scottish parents and grew up in India and Australia before his family moved to the city whose earthy, irreverent and self-deprecating humour he came to embody.

Describing a folk singer as 'someone who stays in bed all day and then goes out at night to sing about work', it was little wonder that he became a favourite folk club compere and a mentor figure to the likes of Billy Connolly, John Martyn and Dick Gaughan.

Hamish's best-loved song 'Cod Liver Oil And The Orange Juice' (written by Ron Clark and Carl MacDougall) – the scurrilous and tragicomic tale of the sweet seduction of Hairy Mary at the Dennistoun Palais – became the most requested song on the British Forces Broadcasting Service in the late 60s and is still a popular turn among the city's young buskers.

Imlach died suddenly on New Year's Day 1996, but not from his fabled allergy to leather. He was often heard to comment that when he woke up after a big night out with his shoes still on, he always seemed to have a headache . . .

DONOVAN

To quote Bob Dylan in the documentary *Dont Look Back*: 'Who is this Donovan?' Allow us to elucidate. Like Lonnie Donegan before him, Donovan Phillips Leitch was born, if not bred, in Glasgow, moving from Maryhill to Hatfield at the age of ten.

As a finger-picking folk troubadour, he suffered in comparison with Dylan but, following his lysergic enlightenment in the mid-60s, he became a key figure in the flower power pop scene, scoring transatlantic hits with 'Sunshine Superman', 'Mellow Yellow' and the totally trippy 'Hurdy Gurdy Man'.

Donovan claims to have influenced Pink Floyd, Led Zeppelin and his friends the Beatles, with whom he hung out in India, and also to have invented Celtic rock. More verifiably, he led the way in high-profile pop star arrests for cannabis possession, scuppering his chances of playing at the Monterey International Pop Festival in 1967.

Donovan remained a conscious believer when it was decidedly unhip to countenance higher planes. In 2007, he returned to the city of his birth to extol the virtues of transcendental meditation with his TM buddy, the great director David Lynch, who filmed the video for his 2010 song 'I Am The Shaman', which was released in May 2021 to celebrate the singer's seventy-fifth birthday.

AC/DC

While it's true that AC/DC formed in Sydney and the Australians like to claim them as one of their own, guitarists Angus and Malcolm Young were born in Glasgow and former lead singer Bon Scott entered this world in 1946 via Fyfe Jamieson Maternity Hospital in Forfar. We'll also point out that Bon actually played the bagpipes on his signature song 'It's A Long Way To The Top (If You Wanna Rock 'N' Roll)'. He managed this despite the fact that his only previous piping experience was as a drummer in a pipe band. The point is, AC/DC are Scottish. We're having them.

Their first Glasgow headline gig was at the City Halls on the Lock Up Your Daughters tour, a title which would raise eyebrows now but was par for the course in 1976. Predictably, the gig was a riot, with Glasgow City Council billing Atlantic Records for damage the fans inflicted on the seats, the curtains and a glass door.

Billy Connolly reckons this Gallowgate mural makes him look like a 'deep-fried Jacobean dandy'.

PURE DEAD GLASGOW

THE HUMBLEBUMS

Glasgow duo the Humblebums might only have merited a footnote in Scottish folk music history if their members Billy Connolly and Gerry Rafferty had not gone on to significantly greater success and, in Connolly's case, national treasuredom as solo artists.

Anderston-born Connolly formed the Humblebums with blue-grass guitarist Tam Harvey in the mid-60s and hit the folk clubs of the nation, garnering at least as much attention for his repartee as for their tunes. Gerry Rafferty joined the jamboree in 1969 and, for a brief period, there were three people in this musical marriage. It was Harvey who jumped.

Rafferty was less accommodating of Connolly's witty interludes. They released two albums, *The New Humblebums* and *Open Up The Door*, after which the new Humblebums became the ex-Humblebums – perhaps for the best, as Connolly himself described his singing voice as resembling 'a goose farting in the fog'. He was also comfortably the second-best guitarist in the Humblebums. It was not unusual at the end of a long day in the studio for Rafferty to send Connolly ahead to the pub to get the drinks in, while he swiftly replaced his bandmate's guitar parts with his own superior efforts.

The Big Yin did not forsake music entirely as he committed to a career in comedy. 'The Welly Boot Song' is practically a public information broadcast, while his parody version of Tammy Wynette's 'D.I.V.O.R.C.E' made it to N.U.M.B.E.R.O.N.E.

Rafferty was on a contrasting trajectory. When his debut album *Can I Have My Money Back?* flopped, he formed Stealers Wheel with his Paisley buddy Joe Egan (an early line-up also featured the redoubtable Rab Noakes) and recorded two albums with US hitmakers Jerry Lieber and Mike Stoller on which he continued to drip disdain for The Man. The Paisley-referencing *Ferguslie Park* was named to emphasise the distance between himself and the London music industry, and he immortalised the clowns and jokers at a record company meeting in 'Stuck In The Middle With You', later used to grisly effect in *Reservoir Dogs*.

He sounded no more chipper on the soft rock classic 'Baker Street' with its iconic saxophone solo most definitely not played by *Blockbusters* host Bob Holness. Several wags, including journalist and broadcaster Stuart Maconie and actual 'Baker Street' saxophonist Raphael Ravenscroft, have claimed responsibility for that enduring urban myth. We do love to print the legend, but that one is beyond the pale.

THE BLUE NILE

Were they enigmatic or did they just not get out much? The Blue Nile, creators of one of the slimmest but most precious catalogues in Scottish pop music, have been described by their biographer Allan Brown as 'a riddle wrapped in an enigma wrapped in a raincoat'.

Though they trod lightly, their footprints are all over the city which they hymned so exquisitely on 'Tinseltown in the Rain' and other melancholic vignettes.

You will find traces at Nico's and the erstwhile Rock Garden, the city centre bars where they worked, in the long-gone Amphora and Saints & Sinners, where they played early gigs, haunting the southside site of the Hermon Baptist Church where they shot the cover of their debut album *A Walk Across The Rooftops*, but mostly in the various Hillhead bedsits where they pondered their high-class, low-budget aesthetic.

Glasgow University students Paul Buchanan, Robert Bell and PJ Moore first convened as McIntyre, named with some deficit of imagination after the John McIntyre Building on campus. They briefly played covers as the White Hats using a drum machine stuck on the 'merengue' setting, but often outnumbered audience members at gigs.

Nigh universal acclaim followed when they emerged as The Blue Nile, but not everyone was convinced – their debut single 'Stay' was slagged off by popular ventriloquist puppet Orville the Duck on the *Saturday Superstore* record review. However, the band were their own harshest critics, allegedly burning master tapes and throwing early

The Blue Nile do Blue Steel: Robert Bell, PJ Moore and Paul Buchanan (left to right) offer their best enigmatic expressions.

singles into the River Kelvin. In the end, these notoriously exacting musicians produced four revered albums and the cult of The Blue Nile received an unexpected boost when they were namechecked on Taylor Swift's song 'Guilty As Sin?' from her 2024 record-smashing *Tortured Poets Department* album.

Buchanan has recorded one solo album, 2012's *Mid Air*, and is sought after as a guest vocalist, though an impromptu performance of a couple of maudlin originals at a fan's house party did require an intervention from the host, saying: 'It's an honour to have you here, but this is a party, mate – play some Slade or get the fuck out.'

BELLE AND SEBASTIAN

No band has captured the leafy appeal of the Dear Green Place quite like Belle and Sebastian. Yet back in 1995, their very creation hung on a shoogly peg as frontman Stuart Murdoch searched doggedly for musical compadres to convey his idiosyncratic vision, hatched on roving bus trips around the city.

The international cult of Belle and Sebastian quickly grew from single-minded roots. Here was a band celebrating tender melodies while their peers were grunging up the city's basement venues; here was a band who refused initially to appear in photographs, instead creating thoughtful or witty tableaux for their record sleeves. No wonder Pete Waterman was confounded when Belle and Sebastian beat his pet project Steps to be voted Best Newcomer at the 1999 Brit Awards.

Their fingerprints are all over the city, from early band meetings in Ashton Lane's Grosvenor Café to their debut gig in a rammed student flat on Renfrew Street, from recording their first two albums in a converted church by Kelvingrove Park to rehearsing in the Hyndland Parish Church Halls where Murdoch lived for a decade as the janitor. Meanwhile, some impish graffiti outside the Byres Road branch of Greggs bakery inspired the title of their song 'La Pastie De La Bourgeoisie'.

They have been generous hosts, curating their own festivals at home and away, in holiday camps and on cruise ships. In June 2004, they helmed the sunny School's Out with Belle and Sebastian in the city's Botanic Gardens. Twenty years later, this most ardently loved outfit headed up the Glasgow Weekender at SWG3.

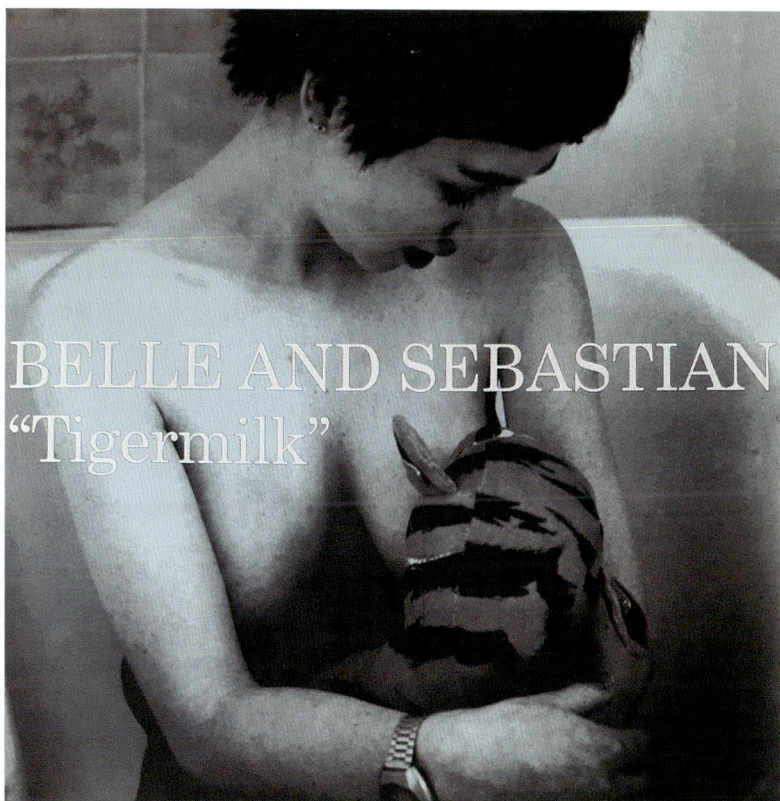

Belle and Sebastian's debut album in vinyl is a sought-after collector's item.

THE PASTELS

Five albums, one soundtrack and one collaboration (with Japanese band Tenniscoats) in forty years – the Pastels may not be the most prolific outfit to emerge from this city of music but they are among the most proactive. Frontman Stephen McRobbie –better known as Stephen Pastel and often simply 'Pastel' – has been described by Sonic Youth frontman Thurston Moore as 'the mayor of the Scottish underground' for his benign influence on indie culture. Over the years, his support of younger artists has been as unwavering as his trademark bowl cut.

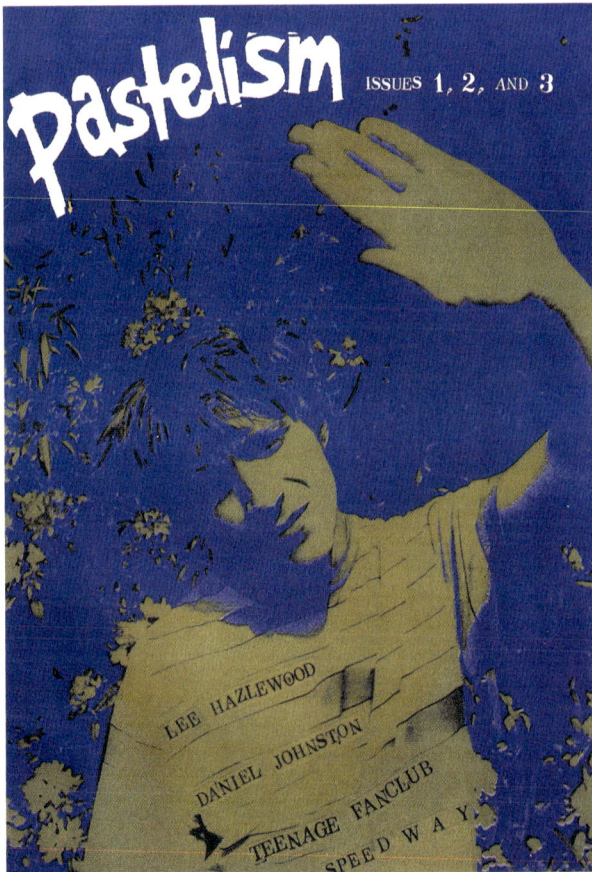

The *Pastelism* fanzine encouraged people to sign up as Friends of the Pastels.

McRobbie and Brian Taylor, aka Brian Superstar, formed the first Pastels line-up with Cheap Gods bassist Martin Hayward and Delmontes drummer Bernice Simpson, soon to be joined by local fanzine writer Annabel Wright, aka Aggi. These self-styled contrarians stepped into the post-Postcard Records breach in the early 80s, invested in the DIY ethos of creating your own scene and eventually released their classic debut album, *Up For A Bit With The Pastels*, in 1987.

For many years, the Pastels have coalesced around McRobbie and Katrina Mitchell, who learned drums on the job, supplemented by visiting players such as Eugene Kelly, Gerard Love and the Shop Assistants' David Keegan, with whom McRobbie had founded Ramones-referencing indie label 53rd & 3rd.

The Pastels now helm their own label, Geographic Music, and McRobbie can be spotted day to day in Monorail Music, the splendid independent record shop he co-founded in 2002. Simpson, meanwhile, works in pharmaceutical marketing. Her clients include Deep Heat, Just for Men and Fisherman's Friend.

GERRY CINNAMON

Before becoming Gerry Cinnamon, the self-made pop star troubadour who became the first Scottish artist to sell out Hampden Stadium (twice), Gerard Crosbie worked as a scaffolder, plumber and chef. Arguably, it is that man-in-the-street quality that has helped propel the singer-songwriter from the open mic nights of Sauchiehall Street to a number one spot in the UK album charts with his 2020 album *The Bonny*.

With a crowd-pleasing patter that reflects his Castlemilk background, and a sartorial style best described as Argyle Street busker on a night out, Gerry has an authenticity that record company marketing campaigns would be at a loss to manufacture. Which is probably just as well as Mr Cinnamon is defiantly DIY and releases all his music through his own Little Runaway Music label. Were a major record label to wave a large cheque in his direction, we suspect they would be sent on their way with some variation of 'get it right up ye' ringing in their ears. He is a belter, that one.

GRAND OLE OPRY

Glasgow's love of country music and a good night out have been two-stepping together at Govan's Grand Ole Opry since 1974. Half a century may have passed since the first Stetson-wearing customer moseyed through the doors, but the club's entertainment formula remains as popular as ever. A night at the Opry is as uniquely a Glaswegian experience as you will find. As well as three sets of live country and western music, regular features include a raffle, bingo and a fast draw simulated shoot-out between aspiring gunslingers in full Western gear.

For those for whom this sounds enticing, it's worth noting that drinks from the Saloon Bar are jaw-droppingly cheap and a visit to the Chuck Wagon can help head off any beer-related munchies at the pass. Cowboy duds are not de rigueur for the curious visitor. Just don't make the rookie error of incorrectly calling *house* at the bingo.

With its social club atmosphere, the Opry may be pure Glasville, but country is not the only music to be heard around these parts. Lloyd Cole, Franz Ferdinand and Celtic Connections have all hitched their horses to the Opry wagon and gigged here.

RADIO CLYDE 261 ALL TOGETHER NOW

Radio Clyde was the first commercial station in Scotland and was launched at 10.30 p.m. on Hogmanay 1973, broadcasting to Glasgow and West Central Scotland from studios in Anderston.

Transmission got underway with a recorded blessing by the Right Reverend Andrew Herron, decreeing that 'at a launching, as we Clyde-siders well know, it is the invariable custom for a prayer to be said invoking God's blessing upon the vessel and upon all who will sail in her', prompting speculation that he may have thought it was a pirate radio station.

Tony Currie, one of the finest voices on radio, kicked off pro-ceedings, playing 'Song Of The Clyde' by Kenneth McKellar, and the first commercial was part of a recruitment campaign for the City of Glasgow Police. Elton John blessed the station by guest-hosting a live four-hour show in 1975, and when Frank Zappa was pictured wearing a tight-fitting red Radio Clyde 261 T-shirt after an interview at the station in 1979, demand for the garments soared. (And they're still being printed by a T-shirt entrepreneur near you, close to half a century later.)

DJ Tiger Tim greets his adoring fans in Shuffles disco, May 1975.

Over the years Clyde has produced many well-known broadcasters, most notably Tiger Tim and Billy Sloan.

Tiger Tim Stevens, born James McGrory, began DJing at the Electric Garden on Sauchiehall Street before hitting on the idea of donning a tiger suit for his audition with Radio Clyde. Tim was a notorious prankster and bum barer. His first show was fittingly titled *The Aff Its Heid Show* and ran on Monday nights. The Tiger was the compere when David Cassidy played at Shawfield Stadium in 1974, but he had his own legion of fans and had to be smuggled in and out of the Radio Clyde studios as hundreds of girls crowded outside hoping to catch a glimpse of him.

Stevens was diagnosed with MS in the 80s and presented his last show, on Clyde 2, in 2010. He was awarded an MBE for his charity work and services to broadcasting in 2006.

Meanwhile, if you were in a band and had a demo tape, Billy Sloan was the man to get it to. He recalls coming back from visits to Glasgow record shops with pockets full of them. He was the first journalist to be inducted into the Barrowland Hall of Fame and currently hosts the *Billy Sloan Show* for BBC Radio Scotland.

Blondie's Debbie Harry proudly clasps her Apollo Theatre statuette.
These trophies were presented to any artist or band who sold out the legendary
venue and were inscribed with the initials SRO – Sold Right Out.

VENUES PAST . . .

THE APOLLO

Stories about the Apollo are legion, from David Bowie fans getting it on in the balcony 'dive-ons' (divans) as a support band called Fumble were playing, to AC/DC's Bon Scott getting locked out of his own gig after going walkabout on Angus Young's shoulders. Hardly the most salubrious of spaces, it was known for its twelve-foot-high stage, meaning that the first few rows of the stalls were the worst seats in the house, and its perilous bouncing balcony, claimed (by Def Leppard's Joe Elliott among others) to move up to eighteen inches under the weight of pogoing fans.

Even though that particular myth was busted when an experiment at a Status Quo concert revealed a mere half-inch of movement, nothing could take the shine (or grime) off the Apollo's legendary status. The venue was so beloved that fans stripped the joint of its fixtures and fittings following its final concert by The Style Council in June 1985. Everyone wanted their own piece of Glasgow gigging history before the walls came tumbling down.

This former 3,500-capacity colossus sat majestically at the top of Renfield Street, first as Green's Playhouse, which opened in 1927 as Europe's largest single-screen cinema, and then for its last twelve action-packed years as the Apollo, its hallowed portals situated between a Mr Chips takeaway and the gentlemen's outfitters West End Misfits. The ground-floor foyer was furnished with pinball machines and arcade games; the top floor became the capacious Clouds Disco and then Satellite City.

Its concert history stretched back to the 60s with plum line-ups such as Jimi Hendrix, Pink Floyd, The Nice, The Move and Amen Corner playing on a single bill in December 1967. David O'List from The Nice filled in for an absent Syd Barrett and the audience were none the wiser. 'It was a reminder you could do the most extraordinary things and get away with it,' recalls Floyd drummer Nick Mason.

Green's then received a maroon makeover in the summer of 1973 and Johnny Cash became the first artist to grace the newly christened Apollo in early September of that year. The same month, a noticeably refreshed Lou Reed played a one-song set, exited in some disorientation and had to be pushed back onstage to finish his show.

Leonard Cohen, in contrast, was so rapturously received in May 1976 that he performed a 35-song set, negotiating outbreaks of 'Flower of Scotland' in the crowd, who were simultaneously celebrating a 2–1 home win in that day's Scotland v. England match at Hampden Park.

Among innumerable classic I-Was-There shows, Buzzcocks were supported by an almighty Joy Division in October 1979. Bob Marley played the only Scottish shows of his career with the Wailers on 10 and 11 July 1980, radiating energy despite being riddled with the cancer that would kill him less than a year later. ABBA played their last ever UK gig in November 1979, with Frida resplendent in a Scotland football shirt and a choir of local schoolkids joining them for 'I Have A Dream'. A year later they immortalised the city in the opening verse of 'Super Trouper', even if it was just a handy rhyme with 'last show'.

The Apollo was a unique gig environment – one that involved dilapidated paintwork, holes in the roof, damp carpets, roosting pigeons and the occasional sewage-related mishap. Van Halen frontman David Lee Roth hailed its 'self-contained ecosystem' and, in later life, the venue was nicknamed the Appalling.

Nevertheless, the Apollo survived a number of threats of closure before the owners decided they could not compete with the newly opened SECC arena by the Clydeside. Conversion to a Mecca bingo hall had been stymied in 1978 by the cost of refurbishment, or maybe by the force of a Save the Apollo petition signed by Eric Clapton and Wings. Bob Geldof of the Boomtown Rats offered his support in the form of an entry in the venue's visitors book, declaring, 'fuck bingo, long live rock'.

The Apollo was truly the epitome of a good old-fashioned scuzzy rock 'n' roll venue but it was also booked in its time for boxing matches, conferences and strike rallies. At one such meeting, an HGV driver got up to address the assembly but broke out a harmonica solo instead. He said he'd always wanted to play the Apollo.

MARYLAND/MAESTRO'S

A gem of Glasgow's music history was uncovered when the CCA – Centre for Contemporary Arts – on Sauchiehall Street underwent major refurbishment in 2001. The original fabric of the building was exposed, including an early nineteenth-century villa which housed various clubs in its day, including the legendary Maryland.

Owned by Bob Gardiner, the club started life as a trad jazz club in the 60s – guests included Acker Bilk, local favourites the Clyde Valley Stompers and George Penman's Jazzmen – before embracing rock 'n' roll and psychedelia. The price of admission ranged from twelve shillings (60p) to fifteen shillings (75p). Pink Floyd played their first Glasgow gig at the Maryland as well as several notable Scottish bands, including the Beatstalkers, Dream Police, and Dean Ford and the Gaylords (who went on to become Marmalade). Fraser Speirs, who is still a highly respected harmonica player in Scotland and a fairly imposing figure, was a member of staff.

When blues legend Muddy Waters played in December 1970, apparently on crutches, his gig was delayed into the wee small hours and patrons were permitted to sleep in the club overnight if they had missed their transport home. Given that the entrance to the club lay halfway up Scott Street, one of Glasgow's steepest, this was probably a wise move, especially since Muddy began the evening by saying, 'I don't know what you're on and you don't know what I'm on but let's have fun.'

The fun was paused in 1971 following a fire on the premises but the club re-opened as Maestro's, *the* place for the city's musicians to play and hang out in the 80s. The space then became the Cotton Club, and finally Lime before being subsumed by the CCA expansion.

ABC

In late 2024, the cultural beacon that was the ABC on Sauchiehall Street was demolished despite heartfelt calls from campaigners to at least retain architect Charles McNair's Art Deco façade. In its time as a gig venue, it hosted star turns by George Clinton, Kendrick Lamar, Janelle Monáe, Bruno Mars, Ed Sheeran and Dua Lipa among many others but this much-loved venue had been keeping the people of Glasgow entertained for 150 years until it became a casualty of the 2018 fire at the Glasgow School of Art.

The original building opened in 1875 and showed dioramas, with the audience viewing historical scenes from a rotating stage. It was then

Guides Phil Eaglesham and Fiona Shepherd
lead a tour outside the former ABC.

converted into Hubner's Ice Skating Palace and hosted Glasgow's first ever film screening in 1896, dubbed 'the rage of the season'. In the twentieth century it was the home of Hengler's Circus, then the Waldorf Palais de Danse before becoming the Regal then ABC cinemas.

Keeping the ABC name, it re-opened as a music venue in 2005 with a gig by Roddy Frame, who hailed its main room as 'big enough to feel important and small enough to feel intimate'. Its signature feature was a rotating disco ball, the largest in the world at two metres in diameter and 250 kilograms in weight.

LOCARNO/TIFFANY'S

The Charing Cross Electric Theatre opened as a cinema in 1910 in a Victorian warehouse building before becoming the Locarno Ballroom in 1926 (see page 35).

Over the years many musicians cut their gigging teeth at the beloved Locarno ballroom, including Maggie Bell – Glasgow's answer to Janis Joplin who is best known for singing the *Taggart* theme tune 'No Mean City'.

On 30 March 1967, The Greatest American Soul Show Ever hit the Locarno when Stax Records presented Otis Redding with special guests Sam and Dave, Arthur Conley, Eddie Floyd, and Booker T. & the M.G.'s. Tickets cost £1 (an advance ticket would set you back seventeen shillings and sixpence). Word had reached the American naval base at Holy Loch, and the sailors were out in force. Legend has it that Otis was repeatedly pulled from the stage by over-enthusiastic fans. This was the first and only time Otis Redding played in Scotland; nine months later he was killed in a plane crash.

By the 70s the Locarno had been renamed Tiffany's and the venue made news in the national music press after Glasgow's infamous Deep Purple riot. Mayhem ensued when the show was moved from the smaller Electric Garden. *Melody Maker* reported that 'an SOS from the staff brought 17 police vans to the scene as frenzied fans blocked the street and hammered at the hall doors'.

In the early 80s, Tiffany's hosted a who's who of post-punk acts including Adam & the Ants, Depeche Mode, an early Duran Duran gig and U2, who played to a half-empty hall on their 1982 Boy tour. The Cure road-tested their new PA system, previously used by Pink Floyd for their Live at Pompeii show, thereby deafening punters in this small venue, which finally closed its ornate doors in 1983 with an Elvis Costello gig.

THE EMPIRE

Empire House, the concrete carbuncle on the corner of Sauchiehall Street and West Nile Street, stands on hallowed ground, for this was the former location of Glasgow's notorious Empire Theatre. Beginning life as the Gaiety Theatre in 1874, it was rebuilt and renamed the Empire in 1897 and was the second largest variety theatre in Britain, attracting the biggest names in showbiz, especially from its 30s heyday onwards. Star turns included Nat King Cole, Judy Garland, Josephine Baker, and Frank Sinatra whose appearance is recounted elsewhere in this book (see page 71).

Jazz legends Django Reinhardt and Duke Ellington went down a storm – there was a rumour that Duke was on a mission to taste haggis

Original Empire Theatre programme dating from August 1955.

while in town (and a local haggis company called McKean's cheekily used his image to endorse their product) – and Louis Armstrong's appearance was described as 'Harlem madness'. Gene Vincent and Eddie Cochran rocked the house on the same bill in 1960.

Ominously the Empire was also known as 'the graveyard of English comedians' – a Glasgow audience would readily let performers know if they found them wanting. Ken Dodd once quipped that 'the trouble with Sigmund Freud was that he didn't have to play second house at the Glasgow Empire after both halves of the Old Firm had lost', and a young Des O'Connor was so overcome with fear when his jokes failed to hit the mark that he faked a faint and had to be carried off stage.

Attendance dwindled as variety shows began to air on television and the Empire closed its doors on 31 March 1963; the audience surely shed tears, but the Empire's spirit lives on.

THE ARCHES

There is something in the brickwork of Glasgow's old industrial spaces which makes ideal environments for clubs, venues and arts ventures. The railway arches under Central Station had been derelict for sixty years when they were dusted out in 1990 to host an interactive exhibition as the centrepiece of the city's European City of Culture celebrations.

When the curtain went down on Glasgow's Glasgow, the street theatre team stayed on, applied for a three-week licence and were granted a year by mistake. And so, with dumb luck and independent spirit, the Arches was born – a gonzo community of theatre makers, club runners, gig promoters and arts administrators who lived and breathed this multi-arts venue for the next twenty-four years.

Massive Attack, the Chemical Brothers and Daft Punk – who loved the place so much they returned as punters – were among the acts who played in the carefree 90s, while the Arches' club nights became the stuff of legend, from dance parties like Pressure and Inside Out run by respected promoters such as Slam and Colours to artsy happenings such as Café Loco and Love Boutique.

In the mid-90s, the queue for visiting superclub Cream was so long that every other club in the city sold out with the overspill. The Arches was able to subsidise their arts and theatre programme from such clubbing revenue – a unique self-sufficient funding model, which was cut off by the city's licensing board following the deaths of two clubbers.

The Arches closed on 15 June 2015, but something of its grit and energy can be found in another industrial venue complex, SWG3, and in its special claim to fame as the birthplace of the time-honoured 'here we fucking go' chant – much to the chagrin of the Slam DJs who would turn the sound down on trigger records in a vain attempt to stamp out the jubilant practice.

THE HELLFIRE CLUB

The name the Hellfire Club has been invoked several times in Glasgow over the years – used by a band, a country music club and, most notoriously, by a gang of fire-raising bounders who laid waste to the Old Tron Church in 1793. Was Jaine Henderson subconsciously channelling this wrecking crew when she dreamed the name for a modest four-track recording and rehearsal studio in Glasgow's West End?

Our favourite Hellfire Club was set up in the early 80s by Jaine's brother David and former Bruce's Records employee Jacqueline Bradley in a tenement basement at 35 Carnarvon Street – handily, just round the corner from Postcard Records HQ, ensuring patronage by a steady stream of Postcard bands. Orange Juice, Aztec Camera, the Bluebells and the Jazzateers, as well as their contemporaries Altered Images, Simple Minds and Bradley's own band Sophisticated Boom Boom, used the Hellfire as a social hangout as much as a studio.

Jools Holland visited its later location in the crypt below CaVa Studios for an episode of *The Tube*, and there is photographic evidence that a young Peter Capaldi frequented the Hellfire long before fighting fictional demonic forces as Doctor Who.

13TH NOTE

When the 13th Note closed its doors in summer 2023, a curtain was (temporarily?) drawn on thirty years of sterling service to Glasgow's grassroots music community. Everybody's gotta start somewhere, but the august likes of Mogwai, Franz Ferdinand and Arab Strap may not have evolved as they did without the independently minded breeding ground that was the 13th Note scene.

In its mid-90s heyday, this vegan café bar was Glasgow's indie living room – in dimensions as much as family atmosphere. Other venues booked young bands on a pay-to-play basis; the 13th Note basement was

13th Note: musical petri dish for Arab Strap, Bis, Mogwai and more.

free to hire and soon attracted a diverse array of upcoming acts with esoteric names such as Urusei Yatsura, Lung Leg and the Yummy Fur.

The emerging scene coalesced around the Kazoo Club and the 99p Club, two of the regular nights run by a dapper young musician called Alex Huntley. 'To get a gig there all you have to do is ask,' noted teen guitar-slinger Sci-Fi Steven at the time. His band Bis were among the first of the Note alumni to break through to wider recognition when they bounced on to *Top of the Pops*, erroneously billed as the first unsigned band to appear on the show. Their sugar rush single 'Kandy Pop' had, in fact, been released on Chemikal Underground, the indie label founded by Note contemporaries the Delgados.

In 1997, the 13th Note moved to King Street from its original home at the top of Glassford Street. Erstwhile Teenage Fanclub drummer Brendan O'Hare was the music booker for a number of years. Note founder Craig Tannock moved on to establish Mono, Stereo, The 78 et al in the same community spirit and Alex Huntley re-emerged as Alex Kapranos, frontman of the suited and booted Franz Ferdinand.

SPLASH ONE

In the summer of 1985, a handbag discotheque just off George Square became the unlikely ground zero for Glasgow's nascent indie scene, as the city's floppy fringes converged for what the screen-printed posters promised would be a Splash One happening 'with a psychedelic punk soundtrack'.

Named after a 13th Note Elevators song, Splash One captured an underground movement on the up. While mainstream Glasgow was in thrall to the pop soul of Wet Wet Wet and their ilk, this stripy T-shirted tribe ransacked Paddy's Market for their retro anoraks and hit the dancefloor of Daddy Warbucks to a pre-recorded soundtrack of 70s post-punk and 60s psychedelia.

Forget lame requests. This was curated music education by committee. Chairman of the board was Bobby Gillespie, who claimed he

Splash One: a Sunday night alternative to *Songs of Praise*.

and his fellow organisers – a collective of seven – compiled each week's playlist on cassette to preserve the integrity of their own vinyl collections. It also handily meant no DJing snafus and no deviations, plus more time for a recreational smoke or two.

Live music was key to the club's appeal. In its time, Splash One hosted seminal shows by Sonic Youth, Wire, Felt and Gillespie's new band Primal Scream, supported by the Pastels, BMX Bandits and, playing their debut gig, the Soup Dragons – the so-called C86 scene of maverick DIY music makers in microcosm.

Like the later and legendary Optimo club night, Splash One took place on Sunday evenings. For one brief year in the mid-80s, this was the place to be for the kids who didn't have school in the morning – and music-loving footballer Pat Nevin, whose fringe could certainly be described as floppy, was occasionally spotted among the anoraks.

GLASGOW FOLK CLUBS

Glasgow's first weekly folk club – the cryptically named **Glasgow Folk Club** – convened in 1959 and soon attracted a regular cohort known as the Broomhill Bums, so called because they would rehearse in Hamish Imlach's Broomhill abode. Other Bums included siblings Ray and Archie Fisher, Josh MacRae of 'Messing About on the River' note and club founder Ewan McVicar. Two of their number were busted for running an illicit still when one plucky imbiber of their 180-proof hooch had to have his stomach pumped at the Western Infirmary.

There were further brushes with the law at the short-lived but celebrated **Clive's Incredible Folk Club**, named for its founder Clive Palmer and his psychedelic folk duo the Incredible String Band. Clive's was an all-night affair which only ran for a few months in 1966 from a fourth-floor room on Sauchiehall Street, until the police intervened to break up all the late-night fun.

Future ISB member Mike Heron described Clive's clientele as 'beatniks and layabouts', some of whom were later to be found at the **Glasgow Folk Centre**, located up a rickety staircase in Montrose Street, where many a Scottish folk legend cut their teeth, from Bert Jansch to Barbara Dickson, Rab Noakes to Phil Cunningham and Aly Bain, not to mention a young John Martyn.

Glasgow's longest running weekly gathering was the **Star Folk Club**, founded in 1978 by singer Arthur Johnstone. Its first of many homes was in the Communist Party HQ on the south bank of the Clyde and it kept the folk faith right through until its end-of-an-era closure in 2022.

SAINT ANDREW'S HALLS

Saint Andrew's Halls, opened in 1877, was a dedicated complex of concert halls, widely regarded as having the finest acoustics in the UK. Located on Granville Street, on the site now occupied by the Mitchell Library extension, the halls were the cultural and political centre of the city for decades until destroyed in 1962 by a fire, believed to have been started by a dropped match at a boxing fixture.

Over the years, prime ministers William Gladstone, David Lloyd George and Winston Churchill spoke in the 4,500-capacity Grand Hall; it was also a regular home for the Scottish National Orchestra with guest conductors including Richard Strauss.

In 1909 the world-famous tenor Enrico Caruso performed for around 3,500 people, US folk legend Pete Seeger amused his audience by chopping wood while performing 'This Land Is Your Land' and in 1961 jazz great John Coltrane's gig, on his first and only UK tour, was considered controversial – one fan asked, 'Are you going to play seriously?', to which an aghast Coltrane apparently replied, 'Ah don't know, man.' And a woman walked out while stating loudly to her mortified companion, 'If this is jazz, you can keep it.' Presumably it was a giant step too far.

KELVIN HALL

Kelvin Hall, which sits opposite the Kelvingrove Art Gallery and Museum on Argyle Street, is currently home to a state-of-the-art fitness centre and the National Library of Scotland Moving Image and Sound Archive. It is still fondly remembered as the onetime home of Glasgow's winter carnival and circus, but from 1956 until the late 70s, it was one of the largest concert venues in the city.

The first musician to appear there was Louis Armstrong, who played on a revolving stage in the middle of the circus ring. The *Herald* reviewer noted 'we saw no hep-cats and only one Teddy boy'.

Glaswegian singer and actress Ella Logan (see page 65), who was touring with Armstrong, bought him a fish supper between sets.

On 24 March 1964 the Jerry Lee Lewis and Gene Vincent Show blew into town and tore the place up, all for eight shillings and sixpence. They were supported by the Animals, who were ignominiously booed off stage. In September, the High Numbers, who went on to become The Who, played at Fab 64 – The Big Beat Show alongside Lulu and the Luvvers.

Scene '67's Big! Big! Beat Show of the Year was a ten-day music festival sponsored by the *Daily Record* and included The Move, Unit 4+2 and culminated with two gigs by the Kinks which were recorded live (see page 77).

Elton John appeared in 1971 and other notable acts who graced the stage include Billy Fury, the Crystals, Tangerine Dream, Captain Beefheart & His Magic Band, Leonard Cohen and Yes.

A CND gig in the mid-80s featured the Pastels and an upcoming young outfit called Wet Wet Wet, sharing a bill for the first and probably last time.

'ARE YE DANCIN'?'

'Are ye dancin'?' The answer to the question inextricably linked with Glasgow's legendary dance halls was 'Are ye askin'?' or 'Naw, it's jist the way ah'm staunin'' – if you were lucky, you might even get a lumber.

Glasgow was dance crazy. During the Second World War the city had at least eighty dance halls and for a certain generation their names still command great affection. Sauchiehall Street boasted the Astoria and the Locarno – which had a convenient room where men could have a free shave and get their suit pressed. The Albert on Bath Street and the Majestic on Hope Street were regular haunts, as was the Barrowland Ballroom in the East End, nowadays famous worldwide as a gig venue (see page 81). Green's Playhouse on Renfield Street opened in 1927 and boasted a double height ballroom, 'brilliant lighting effects' and 'the best sprung dancefloor in Britain'.

The F&F at Partick was a Palais de Danse for three nights a week with the other three reserved for roller-skating, and the Plaza at Eglinton Toll – 'Glasgow's Super Ballroom' – was the epitome of glamour with its central fountain and a bar serving Plaza cocktails.

Ballrooms had resident house bands (and in the 40s big bands were

High heels are kicked off at the Locarno,
September 1962.

all the rage) with famous names often guesting. Band leader Joe Loss was a favourite and described Glasgow as the 'dancingest city in the world'. He recalled, 'One night during the war I found myself in Arnhem. I remember thinking to myself, I've got to get out of here, I'm due in Glasgow at the start of the week.'

All stood still. Ultravox (with Midge Ure on the left) backstage in Philadelphia, 1980.

TOP OF THE POPS

MIDGE URE

Need a guitarist? Keyboard player? Songwriter? Frontman? Producer? Band Aid co-founder? Better give Midge a shout. From Salvation to Ultravox via Slik, Thin Lizzy, Rich Kids and Visage, James 'Midge' Ure has switched musician's roles as deftly as he has surfed scenes from bubblegum pop to punk, rock and New Romantic.

In 2005, Midge was awarded an OBE (Wot? No knighthood!) for his work with Band Aid and Live Aid. However, many think he should also be recognised for his services in popularising pencil-line moustaches and boosting the sales of moody raincoats. Both of which featured heavily in the groundbreaking video to Ultravox's 1981 hit single 'Vienna'. (In fact, Midge's iconic Burberry was a star attraction in 2018's *Rip It Up: The Story of Scottish Pop* exhibition at the National Museum of Scotland.)

Arguably the most famous son of Cambuslang, Midge has left behind the wilder excesses of the rock 'n' roll lifestyle but has not lost his appetite for performing. Now in his eighth decade, he can still be found in the studio and on the road.

BA ROBERTSON

Despite a piecemeal career and many years out of the spotlight, Brian Alexander Robertson has one of the widest cultural reaches of any of his Scotpop peers, penning worldwide hits such as 'The Living Years' for Mike and the Mechanics and 'Wired for Sound' for Cliff Richard, as well as charting in his own right in the early 80s with 'Bang Bang', 'Kool In The Kaftan' and the rollicking Maggie Bell duet 'Hold Me'.

He soundtracked Saturday mornings for a generation of kids with his themes for *Swap Shop* (the later years) and *Saturday Superstore*, hosted his own TV show *BA In Music*, featuring the last filmed interview with Alex Harvey, and starred as a homecoming rock star in the Glasgow-set film *Living Apart Together* – also notable as Peter Capaldi's screen debut.

Arguably, the highlight of his varied CV was writing the droll 1982 Scotland World Cup song 'We Have A Dream', fronted by John Gordon Sinclair, which remains second only to Andy Cameron's 'Ally's Tartan Army' in the Scottish 'pantheon' of World Cup tunes.

The *NME* once dubbed Robertson 'the Ivor Cutler of punk', though he preferred 'the Pam Ayres of the New Wave'. Something of a prophet without honour in his own land, he noted that the Glasgow Apollo was the only venue where he was booed as he stepped *on* to the stage.

ALTERED IMAGES

For a few short years at the turn of the 80s, five young members of the Siouxsie and the Banshees fan club came as close to pop perfection as any Glasgow band ever has. Altered Images took their name from a Buzzcocks record sleeve and got their break as the support act on the Banshees' 1980 Kaleidoscope tour (with teenage roadie Bobby Gillespie in tow), but the release of their debut single 'Dead Pop Stars' was ill-timed following the murder of John Lennon on 8 December 1980.

The effervescent 'Happy Birthday' kicked off a brief run of chart hits, culminating in 'Don't Talk To Me About Love', which was recorded on the same microphone Debbie Harry used for 'Heart Of Glass'. DJ John Peel added backing vocals and whistling to their cover of Neil Diamond's 'Song Sung Blue', later admitting his support of the band was largely predicated on his (understandable) crush on singer Clare Grogan, who also inspired Gary Kemp to write the Spandau Ballet megahit 'True'.

Grogan enjoyed a parallel career as an actor, after being whisked from her waitressing job in West End eatery Spaghetti Factory to star in *Gregory's Girl*. Bassist Johnny McElhone went on to global success in Texas and Grogan's husband Stephen Lironi quit record producing for Happy Mondays and Hanson to run three successful London restaurants.

Grogan has since reconvened a fresh live line-up of Altered Images, and in 2022 released *Mascara Streakz*, their first new album in almost forty years, featuring guest players Lironi, Bobby Bluebell and former Suede guitarist Bernard Butler.

Altered Images' frontwoman Clare Grogan exuding quintessential Glasgow pop chic, *c.* 1981.

EDDI READER

Triple Brit Award winner Sadenia 'Eddi' Reader MBE learned her craft listening to her neighbours singing in the back greens of Anderston and Arden and enjoyed her ringside seat at family gatherings, perched on her granny's piano. She cut her teeth busking round Europe and singing backing vocals for Gang of Four – check out her star turn on 'I Love A Man In A Uniform' – and Eurythmics, before forming the guitarrón-wielding Fairground Attraction with songwriter Mark Nevin.

The group topped the charts with their debut single, 'Perfect', and released one multi-platinum album, *The First Of A Million Kisses*, before breaking up under a cloud in 1990. Many years later, Eddi confused the regulars at the famous Horseshoe Bar karaoke with her impromptu rendition of 'Perfect' – Did you hear that? That lassie was a dead ringer for Reader.

Across a varied solo career, she has acted alongside fellow singer Maggie Bell in the TV series *Your Cheatin' Heart*, presented the BBC Scotland music show *No Stilettos* and carved a path both as a lauded interpreter of Robert Burns' songs and high-profile advocate of Scottish independence.

Reader and Nevin hadn't spoken for over thirty years until Fairground Attraction reformed in 2024 for a second go on the swings with the release of a welcome new album, *Beautiful Happening*.

BILL MARTIN

What does a man have to do to be famous around these parts? Co-writing the Eurovision-winning 'Puppet On A String' for Sandie Shaw in 1967 should ensure more than enough exposure for life-long recognition. You might think that the addition of chart-busting hits for the Bay City Rollers, Cliff Richard and Elvis would be the cherry on top of the celebrity cake. Yet despite these considerable achievements, the late Bill Martin would often lament that 'my songs are household names, but not me'.

Born William Wylie Macpherson, the former Govan dock worker changed his name to Bill Martin after being told that his given name was 'too tartan' for Denmark Street, London's songwriting riposte to Tin Pan Alley. Perhaps, but Martin MBE also reckoned that an upbringing in the cacophonous shipyards made him all the more determined to be heard.

While justifiably proud of his many successes, we suspect that he may not have shouted too loudly about penning 'Back Home', the 1970

England World Cup song. Four years later, he and his songwriter partner Phil Coulter atoned with the release of *Scotland Scotland*, an entire album of songs for Scotland's 1974 World Cup Squad, including their version of 'Back Home' – sung as 'Back Hame'.

STRAWBERRY SWITCHBLADE

As their name suggests, Strawberry Switchblade were a band of striking contrasts. Their backcombed hair, Cleopatra eyeliner and polka-dotted frilly dresses packed a spiky visual punch, while they sang bittersweet pop songs about agoraphobia and nuclear war.

Teenage pals Jill Bryson and Rose McDowall were familiar faces on the Glasgow punk scene before – along with rhythm section Janis Goodlet and Carole McGowan – they formed Strawberry Switchblade in 1981. Paring back to a duo, they recruited Aztec Camera's Roddy Frame to play guitar on their 1983 debut single 'Trees And Flowers'.

Strawberry Switchblade: goth pop with a polka-dot aesthetic.

Their Sibelius-sampling second single, 'Since Yesterday', catapulted them into the Top Ten and on to the cover of *Smash Hits* where they hailed themselves as 'scabby witches from Scotland'. But Strawberry Switchblade were never made for primetime appearances on *Pebble Mill at One* and they split in 1986 after just one eponymous album, tickled by the memory of sitting beside an uncommunicative Prince and his bodyguards at the 1985 Brit Awards. 'We just sat giggling on the other side of the table,' recalls Bryson.

JIMMY SOMERVILLE

It may seem impossible to imagine these days, but Glasgow was not always the enlightened beacon of progressive politics and sexual equality that it would like to be now. In the bands Bronski Beat and the Communards as well as in his solo work, Ruchill-born singer Jimmy Somerville explicitly addressed the more challenging aspects of being young, gay and working-class in 80s Glasgow.

In particular, Bronski Beat's classic 1984 debut single 'Smalltown Boy' was a radical, compassionate, subversive piece of pop work that spelled out the journey many gay people felt forced to make from repressive home-towns to a hopefully brighter future in the big city. It still resonates, with some hailing it a landmark in gay cultural history. In 2024, the fortieth anniversary of the song's release, Paul Flynn, writing in *The Observer*, noted that 'Smalltown Boy' has 'become as indivisible from the story of British gay equality as the imprisonment of Oscar Wilde, the murder of Joe Orton, the work of Derek Jarman or the agit-prop politics of Peter Tatchell'.

TELEVISION PERSONALITIES

It wasn't just Lulu who was all over the telly in the 60s and 70s. A number of Glasgow-born light entertainers took Scottish music to the masses with their regular primetime appearances, not least **Andy Stewart**, who fronted the weekly hoolie that was *The White Heather Club* for a decade from 1958, after 'auditioning' in the gents toilet at the BBC with an impromptu rendition of 'The Muckin' O' Geordie's Byre'.

Stewart went on to host the short-lived *Andy Stewart Show* and toured globally on the back of his hits 'A Scottish Soldier' and the immortal 'Donald, Where's Your Troosers?', even appearing on the *Ed Sullivan Show* not long after those long-haired chancers the Beatles and the Rolling Stones.

He ain't heavy, he's my frontman: Bronski Beat with singer Jimmy Somerville (centre).

Paisley buddy and future Eurovision contestant **Kenneth McKellar** was a *White Heather Club* regular, along with Kirkintilloch songbird **Moira Anderson**, who fronted her own show *Moira Anderson Sings* in the late 60s. But it was **Jimmie MacGregor** with his musical partner Robin Hall who took over the presenter reins from 1964, having already reached a nightly audience of nine million on the BBC's *Tonight* programme. Their somewhat folksy repertoire encompassed the popular and the political, from 'Football Crazy' to 'Pack Your Tools And Go', inspired by the 1971 Upper Clyde Shipbuilders Work-In (see page 103). The ever-twinkly MacGregor marked his ninetieth birthday in 2020 with a Celtic Connections retrospective.

'I got lucky, I suppose' was **Lena Martell**'s modest appraisal of a singing career which started with the big bands at Barrowland. This Bishopbriggs lass went on to share stages with Frank Sinatra and understudy Barbra Streisand on Broadway, but she is best known for her barnstorming cover of a Kris Kristofferson-penned country ballad. 'One Day At A Time' topped the UK charts in 1979, making her the first Scottish woman to score a solo number one and capping a decade when she was rarely off our TV screens as star and host of *Lena Martell Presents*, *Music With Martell*, *Make the Music Speak* and *Lena's Music*.

After many years away from the limelight, wrangling health and financial problems, she returned to performing in her sixties with undimmed vocal talent, including a back-to-her-roots Barrowland concert in 2008.

Lena Martell: the first Scottish woman to score a solo number one.

Travis took a retro approach to their tour bus when promoting their *L.A. Times* album.

CLYDEBUILT MEGASTARS

TRAVIS

In many ways, Travis are the quintessential Glasgow band. Glasgow School of Art background? Check. Numerous fledgling gigs at King Tut's? Check. For a while, they even rehearsed above the Horseshoe Bar on Drury Street, that no-nonsense boozer notable for its enthusiastic karaoke sessions.

Naturally, we will gloss over the fact they had to move to London to really kick-start their rock 'n' roll career. A process that rocketed when they played Glastonbury in 1999 and performed 'Why Does It Always Rain On Me?', the third single from their second album *The Man Who*. Having been dry all day, the heavens obligingly opened for the duration of the televised song and Travis's sales began to soar upwards with a speed that would make well-watered bamboo feel jealous.

Some media commentators mooted that Travis's often wistful, reflective songs may have pioneered a path for Coldplay, but we will forgive them that.

TEXAS

When ex-Altered Images bassist Johnny McElhone first heard Sharleen Spiteri belting out R&B standard 'It Should Have Been Me' at a house party, it was goodbye to her hairdressing job, hello to a blockbusting songwriting partnership. Add in teen whizz guitarist Ally McErlaine and the core of Texas was complete.

Taking their name from the 1984 Wim Wenders film *Paris, Texas*, they evoked its road-movie desert landscape with their slick bluesy debut single 'I Don't Want A Lover', but really hit the commercial heights with their 1997 *White On Blonde* album, partly recorded at Spiteri's home using a cloakroom as a vocal booth, and have since amassed an enviable catalogue of soul-infused pop bangers.

Honoured in summer 2024 with France's Chevalier medallion at the Ordre des Arts et des Lettres, Spiteri – whose paternal grandmother is French – remains a down-to-earth diva who is still partial to an impromptu singsong. At a 2022 Hogmanay hoolie in Braemar's five-star Fife Arms, she joined Dame Judi Dench at the piano for an unlikely rattle through ABBA's 'Waterloo'.

MARK KNOPFLER

The accent may be softly Geordie, but the guitarist, singer and producer Mark Knopfler was born in Scotstoun. As the frontman for Dire Straits, Knopfler was a member of one of the UK's best ever selling bands and, over a hugely varied career as a songwriter, musician and solo artist, he has worked with or for everyone from Bob Dylan to Tina Turner. And we've not even mentioned his extensive charity work or his film soundtracks; most notably 1983's *Local Hero*, which stars our aforementioned pal Peter Capaldi.

Given that he has produced some of the world's most recognisable riffs, it may come as a surprise that Knopfler is left-handed but plays right-handed. 'I hold a guitar like a plumber holds a hammer,' he has said. Well, it works.

LEWIS CAPALDI

On the surface, Lewis Capaldi has it all. Two number one albums, a number one single on both sides of the Atlantic, a Brit Award, Grammy nominations and a natural charm and wit which can't be faked. Hell, he even has his own commercially available pizza: The Big Sexy Cheesy One; yours for £4 at Tesco.

And yet it is not easy being Lewis Capaldi. At the time of writing, the amiable, Glasgow-born singer-songwriter is on an extended break from performing. As covered in his Netflix documentary *How I'm Feeling Now*, Tourette's syndrome, imposter syndrome and anxiety have all plagued Capaldi since his monster hit 'Someone You Loved' topped the UK singles chart in 2019.

In previous decades, the erratic behaviour of assorted rock stars was sometimes worn as a badge of honour. Thankfully, we now live in more enlightened times and when a clearly distressed Capaldi lost his voice during his 2023 Glastonbury performance, an empathetic crowd of Gen Z fans lent their buoyant vocal support and finished his set for him. (Watch the footage if you haven't already; misty-eyed doesn't come close.)

PAOLO NUTINI

Scotland's current Soul Brother No. 1 was born and bred in Paisley, but that hasn't stopped us claiming Paolo Nutini for Glasgow where he has a home on the southside and is regularly spotted in the city's hostelries – M.J. Heraghty's being his choice for a pint of Guinness.

This son of a fish and chip shop owner has spent more than half his life in music, from early gigs at King Tut's, where his parents would buy a hefty wodge of tickets to make sure he had an audience, to a record-breaking run of five sell-out shows at the Hydro in 2022.

Paolo Nutini says of King Tut's: 'It's a classic venue – it's *the* classic venue.'

Nutini was famously discovered filling in for a delayed David Sneddon at Paisley Town Hall. On signing him to Atlantic Records in 2005, legendary label boss Ahmet Ertegun declared, 'I'm as sure about Paolo as I've ever been about any artist I've had.' Nutini was soon singing alongside his labelmates Ben E King and Robert Plant at the Montreux Jazz Festival, a pinch-me moment for a young musician who has since matured into a soul and rock powerhouse with his albums *Caustic Love* and *Last Night In The Bittersweet*.

Nutini is a reluctant star, quietly charitable and not averse to taking the mic at a local karaoke night or making surprise cameos in small clubs. Now that he has made it on his own non-conformist terms, perhaps the Brit Awards might want to revisit his esoteric suggestion for the 2010 ceremony that he duet with Florence + the Machine on a cover of Brian Eno's lyrically enigmatic 1973 number 'Baby's On Fire'.

WET WET WET/MARTI PELLOW

Is it possible for a band's chart-topping, forty-odd year career to be overshadowed by one song? Ask Wet Wet Wet. In 1994, when they released a cover of the Troggs hit 'Love is All Around', the Clydebank soul pop outfit had already had several international hits. 'Love Is All Around', included on the soundtrack of the romcom *Four Weddings and a Funeral*, eclipsed all of them and spent fifteen weeks at the pinnacle of the UK charts. An extended period which helped cement the Wets' rep as one of the UK's most commercially successful bands. The less charitably minded, or indeed jealous, may have concluded that those fifteen weeks felt like we were all being slowly buried alive.

After several splits and dormant periods, Wet Wet Wet are still touring, albeit without most of the original members, including former frontman Marti Pellow. Born Mark McLachlan, Pellow's turbulent personal life became tabloid fodder for a while. However, all is now on an even keel and the man with the brightest teeth in showbiz is forging a solo musical career while simultaneously carving his own path in musical theatre.

Several decades after 'Love Is All Around' triumphed, the very words 'I feel it in my fingers, I feel it in my toes' may still make many people feel like reaching for their ear protectors, but even the most curmudgeonly could not deny the Wets their undoubted popularity.

DEACON BLUE

Teacher, youth worker and aspiring singer-songwriter Ricky Ross moved from his native Dundee to Glasgow in his mid-twenties with no great plan to form a group. A few years later he was fronting Deacon Blue: for many, the quintessential Glasgow band, who tap into a special energy whenever they play a home concert and who were natural headliners at the city's largest ever musical gathering, The Big Day, in 1990 (see page 76).

Ross's affinity for storytelling, romance and social justice chimes well with his fellow denizens. Deacon Blue's signature tune, 'Dignity', was inspired by watching street sweepers from his Pollokshields flat and went on to be voted the Greatest Scottish Song of all time in a 2020 Radio Clyde poll.

The band played their earliest gigs at the Midas on St Vincent Street and the Fixx on Miller Street and signed their record deal by the Finnieston Crane, once operated by vocalist Lorraine McIntosh's uncle. This shipbuilding landmark featured on the evocative Oscar Marzaroli cover shot of their cherished debut album, *Raintown*, released in spring 1987.

In other tributes to the Dear Green Place, the loose narrative of their third album *Fellow Hoodlums* was 'set' in the city centre, 2020's *City of Love* was recorded at the Gorbals Sound studio, not far from where some of St Valentine's bones were said to have been sequestered in St Francis Church, and their latest album, marking forty years as a band, is named after mighty boulevard *The Great Western Road*.

Ross and McIntosh have forged parallel careers in broadcasting and acting and released a gorgeous Americana album as McIntosh Ross. *The Great Lakes* was recorded in Los Angeles in 2009, but its cover photograph was pure Glasville, taken through the window of the historic Val D'Oro chippie on London Road (see page 105).

DEL AMITRI

Despite recording a couple of sessions for John Peel, scoring Single of the Week in *Sounds* for their 1983 debut 'Sense Sickness' and featuring on the cover of *Melody Maker* prior to the release of their debut album, Del Amitri were never cool. According to frontman Justin Currie, they aspired to sound like a cross between Television and Captain Beefheart with Beatles harmonies: 'Of course, we ended up sounding nothing like that.' Their debut gig at Bearsden Burgh Hall, arranged by their drummer, turned out to be a benefit for the Scottish Liberal Party. Never. Cool.

Del Amitri: backs to the wall but still gigging.

But they were, and are, hugely popular, even if it took almost a decade from that first fateful show to score their breakthrough hit. 'Nothing Ever Happens' was the world beyond Glasgow's introduction to the self-deprecating wit of Justin Currie, which arguably reached peak bathos (sic) in the form of Del Amitri's official 1998 Scotland World Cup anthem 'Don't Come Home Too Soon'. Not long afterwards, the band were dropped by their label and went on hiatus for over ten years. Their next album, released almost twenty years later, was called *Fatal Mistakes*.

The drollery continues, but for how long? Currie revealed in early 2024 that he has Parkinson's disease, a condition he anticipates will eventually rob him of the ability to perform live, yet which he writes about with much wit and insight in his book *The Tremolo Diaries*. He has nicknamed the tremor in his hand Gavin.

BIFFY CLYRO

'Mon the Biff!' This rock 'n' roll rallying cry has rung out over Scotland and beyond for the past quarter century, with more voices adding to the fanfare as Biffy Clyro made their slowburn ascent through the ranks to become the nation's favourite rock band.

Frontman Simon Neil and twin brothers James and Ben Johnston, hailing from Irvine and Kilmarnock respectively (close enough to claim for Glasgow in our keen opinion), released their debut EP *thekidswhopoptodaywillrocktomorrow* on Glasgow independent label Electric Honey Records (see **Record Labels**, page 109) in 2000, a punky prototype for the idiosyncratic and influential melange of metal, prog and melodic rock to follow. Three of their albums to date have topped the charts and they scored a number one single (sort of) when their lighter-waving ballad 'Many Of Horror', retitled 'When We Collide', was released as Matt Cardle's *X Factor* winner's single in 2010.

Biffy are habitual advocates of Scotland's 'taps aff' tradition of stripping to the waist whatever the weather at their many outdoor enormo-gigs, though in recent years this sharp-dressed threesome have taken to keeping their couture shirts on at least some of the time.

They remain playfully opaque on the origins of their name – only they know if Biffy Clyro is a seventeenth-century Finnish footballer, a concatenation of the name of the spy who inspired Ian Fleming to create James Bond and a childhood holiday destination in Wales or a Spoonerism

Biffy's Simon Neil demonstrates 'taps aff' at Open Flair Festival, 2017.

of Cliffy Biro, part of a range of Cliff Richard merchandise they dreamed up at school. 'We weren't high at the time,' insists Neil. 'There's just not a lot to do in Ayr.'

CHVRCHES

Synth pop power trio Chvrches (pronounced 'churches') chose their stylised name to make it easier to find them online – a shrewd move as they quickly blew up all over the internet in 2012 with their debut track 'Lies'. Within a year, they were performing on *Late Night with Jimmy Fallon* and supporting Depeche Mode in the US.

All three members – Lauren Mayberry, Iain Cook and Martin Doherty – had history in Glasgow indie bands such as The Twilight Sad, Aereogramme and Blue Sky Archives, but Chvrches achieved international success on a blockbusting level. Mayberry, in particular, was in the eye of the social media storm, fire-fighting misogyny and emerging as an eloquent advocate for LGBT and environmental causes. She has been described as 'the punk rock Joan of Arc of pop' by onetime Chvrches producer, Dave Stewart of Eurythmics.

This former section editor at *The List* and founder of feminist collective TYCI (standing for . . . something a bit rude) now lives in Los Angeles but still counts Glasgow as the place where 'all my proper, proper pals are'. With Chvrches on hiatus, she has struck out solo with a 2024 debut album *Vicious Creature* and an all-female backing band. 'When you have this opportunity, better make 15-year-old you proud,' she says, 'otherwise what's the point?'

ACCEPTABLE IN THE 80s

Legend has it that in mid-80s Glasgow you only had to walk down the street carrying a guitar with a nonchalant air or be spotted grooming your quiff in hipster hangouts the Rock Garden, Nico's and the Equi Café to be collared by eager beaver representatives of London labels waving lucrative record deals. Was Sade really poised to join jazzy ensemble the French Impressionists, or did Lloyd Cole just make that up for effect?

Regardless, this was an extraordinarily fertile time for the city's musicians, especially those of a pop soul bent. Success bred success and the chartbound likes of Del Amitri, Texas and Wet Wet Wet were the tip of an immaculately turned-out iceberg.

The Bluebells were among the first off the blocks, although they had to wait until the early 90s to score a number one with a reissued 'Young At Heart' and lark around in top hat and tails on *Top of the Pops*. **Hue & Cry**, fronted by brothers Pat and Greg Kane, were/are altogether more serious, combining socialist politics with mid-Atlantic soul on their most enduring song, 'Labour Of Love', while the sublime **Lloyd Cole & the Commotions** captured the leafy, literary romance of the West End a good decade before Belle and Sebastian.

The Bathers and **the Big Dish** followed The Blue Nile's lead in classy pop, **the Silencers** and the **Kevin McDermott Orchestra** brought a rootsy edge to the scene, while **Trashcan Sinatras**, hailing from non-leafy Irvine, and **the Pearlfishers** were late bloomer outliers who looked to the 60s for inspiration.

Slick pop operators **Love & Money** and **Hipsway** have both reformed in the last decade to reap the enduring love. L&M frontman **James Grant** has also formed a wise-cracking songwriters' powwow with Teenage Fanclub's Norman Blake and Suede's Bernard Butler, while erstwhile Hipsway/Texas keyboard player **Craig Armstrong** has achieved global success as a composer, scoring films for Baz Luhrmann and Oliver Stone, and as an orchestral arranger for artists from Massive Attack to Madonna.

F·F·S

FRANZ FERDINAND • SPARK

INDIE GODS

FRANZ FERDINAND

To anyone outside Glasgow's grassroots music community, Franz Ferdinand appeared to pop up fully formed in 2004 with their stomping indie anthem 'Take Me Out'. Frontman Alex Kapranos and original drummer Paul Thomson were already gig-hardened veterans of various local bands – the Blisters, the Karelia, the Yummyfur, Pro Forma – but it wasn't until they teamed up with bass novice Bob Hardy and guitarist Nick McCarthy, recently arrived from Munich, that the stars aligned and the self-styled 'new Scottish gentry' swaggered forth to international success and a 2004 Mercury Prize win for their self-titled debut album. Five more albums – six if you include *FFS*, their inspired collaboration with the enigmatic Sparks – and some line-up changes later, Franz Ferdinand are still a live force to be reckoned with.

They were – and remain – glamorous but grounded, rhapsodising their home city with tales of early happenings in their Chateau HQ – in reality, a dilapidated warehouse on Bridge Street and then an abandoned jail in Bridgeton. They have hailed the Transmission Gallery's legendary launch parties in the lyrics of 'Do You Want To' and written songs about their Glasgow pals Michael and Jacqueline. The former is musician and record label owner Michael Kasparis, whose suggestive dancing at a club inspired the homoerotic hit, while the latter is SNP councillor Jacqueline Cameron, whose encounter with a flirtatious Ivor Cutler was immortalised in the song that bears her name.

FEEDBACK AND FUZZ GUITARS

According to the title of their 'all warts' 2024 autobiography, the **Jesus and Mary Chain** were *Never Understood*. But, despite chaotic appearances to the contrary, the Reid brothers were clear on their pop mission, forged in their early 80s East Kilbride bedroom on a Portastudio bought with their dad's redundancy pay: to make music as important as that of the punk bands, psychedelic outfits and classic girl groups which they idolised. Younger brother Jim lost the coin toss and became the singer, William the feedback-laced guitarist, with bassist Douglas Hart on three-string bass and local scenester Bobby Gillespie bashing a pared-back drumkit.

The Mary Chain were not long for East Kilbride, but they made an instant impact with their debut single 'Upside Down' and a succession of riotous twenty-minute gigs. Gillespie would soon have to choose between guesting with his pals or committing fully to his own group, **Primal Scream**. They may have presented as jangle pop fops but, having formed in the shadow of Hampden Park, the Scream based their live formation on Jock Stein's strategy for the Scottish football team in the 1967 European Cup. According to Gillespie, every gig should be 'a commando raid on the soul'.

The two bands came together in October 1984 at one legendary Creation Records night at Glasgow's Venue, just off Sauchiehall Street, supported by the Pastels and Meat Whiplash. They may not have been fancied to see out the year, never mind the decade, but their enduring, hugely influential albums, *Psychocandy* (1985) and *Screamadelica* (1991), soon paved the way for longevity, abundant catalogues and elder indie statesman prestige.

REGULAR MUSIC

presents

The JESUS and MARY CHAIN

at BARROWLAND, GLASGOW
on FRIDAY, 11th SEPTEMBER, 1987

Ticket £5.00 in Advance
Doors open at 7.30 p.m.

№ 70

Management reserve the right of admission - over 18 s

MOGWAI

Mogwai, one of the most respected groups ever to emerge from Glasgow, have come a long way since the Britpop-baiting days of their infamous 'blur: are shite' T-shirts.

Their acclaimed soundtrack work on Douglas Gordon's *Zidane*, Mark Cousins' *Atomic* and the French TV series *Les Revenants* was some way off when they formed as callow noiseniks in the mid-90s. Named after the cute creatures which became Gremlins, they have always had musical teeth and a single-minded streak, sacking one-time drummer Brendan O'Hare for the crime of talking through an Arab Strap concert.

Their humour manifests in irreverent song titles, such as 'Glasgow Mega-Snake', 'Secret Pint', 'Coolverine' and the prescient 'George Square Thatcher Death Party' from 2011's *Hardcore Will Never Die, But You Will*, if not in the names of their bespoke limited-edition single-cask whisky (RockAct81W) and rum (rockact81r).

The band remain pleasantly surprised at their indie veteran status. In 2021, following a hard-fought but genial chart battle with grime rapper Ghetts, Mogwai scored their first number one with their tenth album *As The Love Continues*, prompting the gush that 'we want to thank everyone at Rock Action Records – both of you'.

BELLSHILL BAND(IT)S

According to Teenage Fanclub frontman Norman Blake, Sean Dickson was The First Guitarist In Bellshill. There wasn't much going on in their humdrum North Lanarkshire town, so they made it happen. Along with their mutual friend Duglas Stewart they planted the roots of an indie pop family tree with three particularly sturdy branches – **Teenage Fanclub**, the Dickson-fronted **Soup Dragons** and Stewart's rag-tag cult heroes, the **BMX Bandits**.

Other key players, including Jim McCulloch, Joe McAlinden and Francis Macdonald, met on the busking trail. Briefly, there were bands called the Faith Healers and the Child Molesters, then the considerably more fragrant Pretty Flowers, and then the BMX Bandits, who boldly waved their freak flag with debut single 'E102'.

Blake's next band, the Boy Hairdressers, evolved into Teenage Fanclub. No amount of self-deprecating attitude could disguise the skills of their songwriting triumvirate of Blake, Raymond McGinley and

Bellshill cult heroes BMX Bandits strike a pose. Sole permanent member
Duglas T. Stewart gives a thumbs-up on the right.

erstwhile member Gerry Love. Their second album *Bandwagonesque* jostled with Nirvana's *Nevermind* at the top of the 1991 Best Of polls. Kurt Cobain proclaimed the Fannies his favourite band.

By this point, the Soup Dragons had gone from debut flexi-disc (how indie is that?) and inaugural Peel session (with train fare to London subsidised by John Peel himself) to sharing Wham!'s management and Top Ten single status with their loose cover of the Rolling Stones' 'I'm Free' – Dickson sang his 'free' version from memory.

Stateside success followed and the band were invited to play Prince's Glam Slam Club where the Purple One reportedly boogied on down to 'Divine Thing' at the soundcheck. They were further bound together by a pressing plant mistake when thousands of vinyl copies of Prince's *LoveSexy* were pressed with one side of the Soup Dragons' debut album *This Is My Art*.

The band split in the mid-90s but reformed in 2023 for a number of shows. Their Bellshill buddies prevail. The BMX Bandits released their beautiful *Dreamers On The Run* album in 2024, while the beloved Teenage Fanclub look set on challenging the title of their most recent album, *Nothing Lasts Forever*.

The inimitable actress and singer Ella Logan: wanted for crimes against bagpipes.

CULT HEROES

ELLA LOGAN

FBI Teletype: *'Ella Logan, Re Los Angeles teletype June thirteen. Bureau desires discreet full coverage of Logan's activities in New York City. Arrange for search of personal effects upon departure.'*

Standing at four foot eleven, Ella Logan was short of stature but a big cause for concern to the FBI, who suspected the singer and actress of having communist ties.

Born in Glasgow in 1913, she made her stage debut just before her third birthday at the Grand Theatre in Paisley. By her mid-teens she was performing in nightclubs and cabarets across Europe and just before her seventeenth birthday she cut her first recording with the Jack Hylton Orchestra. Ella moved to the USA in the 30s where she began a successful stage career on Broadway and went on to appear in several movies.

During the Second World War she travelled to Italy to perform for the troops, who dubbed her 'the Queen of the Fifth Army'. Post-war she became a person of interest to the FBI. Although no proof was ever found to support the allegation she was a Russian courier agent, the FBI kept a file on her from 1945 to 1961, curtailing her career.

She returned to Broadway in 1947 to star in the original production of *Finian's Rainbow*. Performing ran in the family. Logan's nephew was legendary entertainer and impresario Jimmy Logan and her niece, esteemed jazz vocalist Annie Ross, spent some of her childhood living with her notorious auntie in Beverly Hills.

Ella Logan died in 1969. Her obituary in the *New York Times* described her as 'a vocal volcano'.

JET MAYFAIR

Jet Mayfair, aka Glasgow's Greatest Nightclubber, was a local superhero. By day he was mild-mannered British Rail labourer Stanley Frossman but by night he donned his legendary gold lamé suit and shades to throw spectacular shapes on the dancefloor.

Such was the affection he commanded in 70s clubland that admission and drinks were always free. Venue owners treated him as a lucky mascot. Apollo impresario Frank Lynch often sought him out to inject some razzamatazz. On one occasion he flew around the venue on a high wire dressed as a Christmas fairy.

Jet met many of the visiting musicians and jammed with some. He counted Noddy Holder among his fans and was uniquely honoured with a Lifetime Achievement Award by the Glasgow branch of the British Entertainment and Disco Owners' Association in 2006 before heading to the big nightclub in the sky in 2017.

MR SUPERBAD

Freddie Mack is fondly remembered as the host of Radio Clyde's *Mr. Superbad Boogie Show* but his life prior to arriving in Glasgow in 1979 was the stuff of biopics.

Mack grew up on a cotton plantation in South Carolina. His family moved to Brooklyn where future heavyweight champion Floyd Patterson was a childhood friend. They learned to box together and, in 1952, Mack served as Patterson's reserve at the Helsinki Olympics. At one point, he placed third in the world light-heavyweight rankings and even sparred with Muhammad Ali.

Next stop, Hollywood, where he played one of the slaves carrying Elizabeth Taylor into Rome in the epic *Cleopatra*. Small parts in *The Great Rock 'n' Roll Swindle* and *Taggart* followed.

On moving to the UK, Freddie began a new career as an R&B singer with the Freddie Mack Sound. In 1974 he was signed to K-Tel Records as Mr. Superbad and sang vocals on the single 'Kung Fu Man' by Ultrafunk. Coming full circle, he founded the Scottish Boxing Hall of Fame in 2001, but it was his rich groovy timbre on the radio airwaves that was the real knockout.

THE VASELINES

When Eugene Kelly and Frances McKee formed the Vaselines in 1986 in a spirit of DIY mischief, they were not to know that their witty, scrappy indie missives would resonate with a certain disaffected young musician in the US Pacific Northwest. Having already claimed Teenage Fanclub as his favourite band, the ever fervent Kurt Cobain would go on to declare the Vaselines his 'favourite songwriters in the whole world' and cover their song 'Jesus Doesn't Want Me For A Sunbeam' on Nirvana's blockbusting live album *MTV Unplugged*. Cobain and his wife Courtney Love even named their daughter Frances Bean after McKee.

By this point, the Vaselines had split but Kelly's new band, Captain America, supported Nirvana at their sole Glasgow show at the Queen Margaret Union. He also shared a mic with Cobain at the 1991 Reading Festival when Nirvana covered the Vaselines' 'Molly's Lips', a gleeful tune inspired by Kelly's childhood habit of kissing his TV screen whenever Scottish actress Molly Weir made an appearance.

The duo reformed in 2008, releasing two more albums of irreverent garage pop, and touring as the mood takes them. The multitasking McKee was last spotted leading the yoga classes on deck at Belle and Sebastian's Boaty Weekender festival cruise. Namaste!

IVOR CUTLER

Adored by fans including John Lennon, Billy Connolly, Franz Ferdinand and KT Tunstall, there is nobody quite like Ivor Cutler, the great Glaswegian sage, storyteller and songwriter who starred as lugubrious bus conductor Buster Bloodvessel (not to be confused with the big ska guy with the tongue trouble) in the Beatles' *Magical Mystery Tour* movie. Cutler went on to record the 1967 LP, *Ludo*, with Beatles producer George Martin. He clocked up more John Peel sessions than any other act (apart from Peel's beloved The Fall), and could often be seen on late-night television shows performing his odd odes on his trusty harmonium.

Born in Govan in 1923, Cutler claimed that the birth of his younger brother was the catalyst for his artistry: 'Without that I would not have been as screwed up as I am and therefore not as creative.' On leaving school he worked as an apprentice fitter at Rolls-Royce before joining the RAF in 1942 to train as an air navigator where he was grounded for 'dreaminess'.

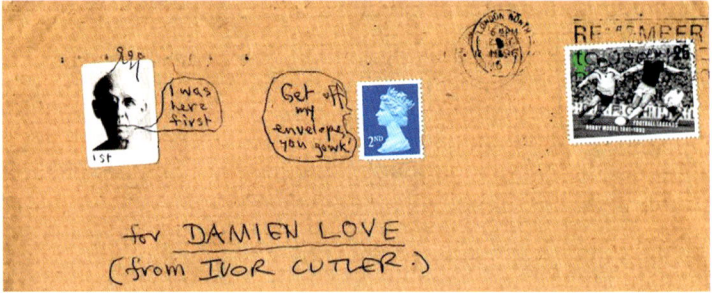

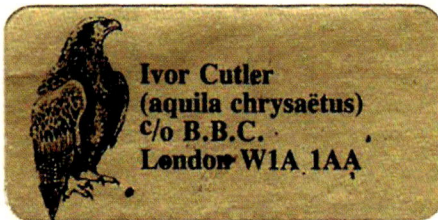

Witty missives from the idiosyncratic cosmos of
Ivor Cutler, who was known to hand out Post-It notes
bearing gnomic messages to strangers in the street.

Years after his death in 2006, he still commands great affection in his hometown, where he has been celebrated in the 2014 theatre production *The Beautiful Cosmos of Ivor Cutler* and at a massed tribute concert at the 2020 Celtic Connections festival, featuring musicians from across Scotland's indie and folk fraternities.

Once asked in an interview if he had anything to declare he replied: 'I'm a spore from outer space, landed on the wrong planet. Somewhere, there's a planet where some spores are waiting for me to turn up, so they can get on with their dinner.'

SYDNEY DEVINE

Sydney Devine's uniquely Glaswegian take on easy listening country and western music made him an institution in the city, but the man affectionately dubbed Steak and Kidney began his career as a teenage whistler – a talent which came in handy when he quelled a rock 'n' roll riot at Paisley Town Hall with his chirruping.

Next, billed as the 'Tartan Rocker', he went on tour with the *White Heather Club*. Following a performance at an American military base in Germany, he was informed mysteriously that 'Mr Presley has been watching you', though it was never confirmed that Elvis was in the building.

In 1957 the *Daily Record* launched a competition to find Scotland's answer to Tommy Steele, Sydney entered and came second, only pipped at the post by Alex Harvey. Sydney paid up his first guitar from McCormack's, 'half a crown down and a change of address', and he later played on Andy Stewart's 'Donald, Where's Your Troosers?'.

In 1974, Glasgow's own rhinestone cowboy recorded his signature song 'Tiny Bubbles' and played at the Pavilion Theatre for the first of forty-five – count 'em – consecutive years. Those November concerts attained legendary status in Glasgow, often with generations of the same families in attendance.

He helmed two shows for Radio Clyde in the 70s, signing off each broadcast with the catchphrase 'Get the kettle on, Shirley'. He was mercilessly mocked for his singing style and was the butt of frequent jokes. For example, 'What's got a hundred legs and three teeth? The front row of a Sydney Devine concert.' Maybe so, but Steak and Kidney MBE had the last laugh, selling an estimated 15 million albums across a seven-decade career.

The Pavilion Theatre, Sydney Devine's favourite stomping ground
for almost half a century.

NOTABLE GIGS

SINATRA AT THE GLASGOW EMPIRE

In some ways 1953 was a very good year for Frank Sinatra. His new contract with Capitol Records and his Oscar-winning performance in *From Here to Eternity* were soon to usher in his imperial phase as he landed in Glasgow in early July for a week-long residency at the Empire Theatre – where he was supported by variety turns including jugglers the Three Lederers and roller-skating act Williams and Sand.

On arrival in the city, the man dubbed 'Swoonatra' reportedly ran a 'small gauntlet of fans' to conduct an informal press reception in the foyer of the Central Hotel, revealing – as it turned out, erroneously – that he saw his future in comedy roles rather than music. His repartee was sparkling when he took the stage later that night, and his voice sublime, lubricated by a tea break behind the footlights. 'It helps the cords,' he claimed.

He returned to the city only once, exactly thirty-seven years later, to play Ibrox Stadium on 10 July 1990. His support act, Shettleston-born veteran vocalist Carol Kidd, performed barefoot, a tradition upheld since her debut at the Glasgow Jazz Festival when, in her stage fright, she put her shoes on the wrong feet and kicked them off, never to be encumbered onstage again.

Kidd recalled that Sinatra's soundcheck consisted of four words – 'come fly with me'. The event was fraught with ticketing issues, but Sinatra delighted the 11,000-strong audience by going walkabout for 'Strangers in the Night' and referring to himself as 'the American Andy Stewart'. The feeling was mutual with Ol' Blue Eyes saying afterwards, 'In all my time in showbusiness I have never had such a stupendous feeling. I have never been so moved by anything in my life before.'

THE BEATLES IN GLASGOW

What is the best city you've ever played?

John: I don't know.

Ringo: It's impossible, you know.

Paul: Actually, one of the wildest audiences was, I think, Glasgow.

Ringo: Glasgow, Scotland.

– Beatles press conference, 22 August 1964, Vancouver

When promoters Andi Lothian and Albert Bonici first booked an unknown young group from Liverpool for a mini tour of Scotland's provinces in January 1963, audiences were paltry. Still, they thought the Beatles had something and gambled on booking them again. By the time they returned for their first Glasgow headline, at the Glasgow Concert Hall (located at 625 Argyle Street) on 5 October 1963, the Beatles had topped both the singles and album charts. Lothian reckoned that this time he should provide security and arranged for 'a load of boxers' to act as bouncers.

There were two performances. By the time the later concert was due to begin, audience impatience was growing, and police demanded the gig start early. But the bouncing boxers were nowhere to be found. As hysterical girls rushed the stage, a Radio Scotland interviewer asked what was happening. Lothian replied, 'Don't worry it's only . . . BEATLEMANIA' and later recalled that finally from the back of the hall 'forty drunken bouncers appeared, rolling down the aisle, like the Relief of Mafeking'.

A council representative was less impressed, saying: 'This kind of behaviour is not going to be tolerated in Glasgow Concert Hall. There was so much shouting and screaming that, I am told, the Beatles group could not be heard. The balcony was actually shaking with all the pandemonium that was going on.'

There was no less mania on the four occasions when the Beatles played the Odeon Cinema on Renfield Street. In Oct 1964, mounted police charged at ticketless fans who had overturned a car, while inside the venue trainee managers got a crash course in crowd control with the instruction that 'you've got tae keep the wimmin off the band'. One attendee likened the sight of fainting fans in the foyer to the aftermath of the battle scene in *Gone with the Wind*.

DANCING ON RENFIELD STREET

The Tamla Motown Revue blew into Glasgow for two shows on 1 April 1965. Gracing the stage at the Odeon on Renfield Street were the Supremes, Smokey Robinson and the Miracles, Martha and the Vandellas, Earl Van Dyke and a fourteen-year-old Stevie Wonder. Hot on the heels of their smash hit 'Yeh Yeh', Georgie Fame and the Blue Flames were added to the bill to boost sluggish ticket sales for the twenty-date tour.

The tour was gruelling. Mary Wilson remembers 'we would always get fish 'n' chips because that was so new for us, eating out of a newspaper was very exciting, but I wasn't that thrilled about the English food . . .' The waxy toilet paper wasn't too popular either.

Tamla Motown All Stars: Detroit's finest, with Stevie Wonder (front row, centre) blissfully unaware of the imminent loss of his suit.

Could this in fact have been the final straw? The tour was jeopardised when the artists staged a wildcat strike and refused to perform until they were paid – money had to be wired from Detroit.

Further drama ensued when Stevie Wonder's suit was nicked between sets, handed over in good faith to someone backstage calling out 'suits for cleaning, suits for cleaning'. It was never returned. Music industry veteran Keith Harris, who has represented Stevie Wonder since the 70s, said, 'There's somebody in Glasgow with a Little Stevie Wonder suit. I hope they appreciate it.'

BEAT BEDLAM IN GEORGE SQUARE

There may be no such thing as a free lunch – a free lunchtime concert is another matter. On 11 June 1965, fans of local combo the Beatstalkers turned up in droves to George Square to grab a piece of the gratis action. The city fathers anticipated attendance by around two hundred harmless pop fans; estimated numbers edged closer to seven thousand.

Although dubbed 'the Scottish Beatles', the quintet were unprepared for the resulting hysteria, described in the *Evening Times* as 'beat bedlam in the square'. A local razor gang were drafted in as security with mounted police reinforcements, but the gig was abandoned after half an hour when the stage collapsed. The band members were swiftly hustled into the City Chambers for their own safety. With fans in hot pursuit, they escaped the building via secret passageways and were photographed afterwards looking a tad shellshocked.

The Beatstalkers were a genuine, if short-lived, Scottish pop sensation. Their record company newsletter cautioned that 'they walk down Sauchiehall Street at their peril'. Fans had to be prised off the landing gear of their plane. They sold 80,000 copies of their debut single 'Ev'rybody's Talking 'Bout My Baby' in Scotland alone, but fell foul of chart return rules and failed to score a hit. Moving to London, they recorded a handful of songs penned by a young David Bowie, who sang backing vocals on 'Silver Tree Top School For Boys', but wider success was elusive and the band spit in 1969. They reunited for a sell-out Barrowland show in 2005. On this occasion, the stage survived.

SAHB IN THE FRAME AT THE APOLLO

Arguably the most fondly remembered Apollo gigs are the three Christmas dates played by the Sensational Alex Harvey Band in 1975, the recollection of which is enough to make grown men tearful. The programme for those shows contained the typically Glaswegian guidance to 'wish the stewards a happy Christmas, don't pish in the water supply and have a stoatin' New Year'.

One attendee recalled frontman Alex Harvey performing the audience favourite 'Framed'. Or 'fram-ed' as Alex liked to pronounce it. The song tells the sorry tale of a street punk fitted up for a crime he allegedly didn't commit. A role which Alex revelled in.

When the song reached its climax, our hero was on his knees, picked out by a spotlight as he howled out the lines, 'I was fram-ed, I never did nothing.' Instantly from the darkness of the stalls came a withering response from an aggrieved punter, 'Aye, you did. You shagg-ed ma sister.'

BIG COUNTRY ROCK THE NEW YEAR

Backstage at Barrowland, tucked away by some unprepossessing lighting switches, is a piece of priceless graffiti declaring: 'These points are a gift from Simple Minds to Big Country! Happy New Year!' Simple Minds were the first band to play Barrowland on its revival as a gig venue in November 1983 (see page 81), but they knew that Fife's finest were next in line, booked to play two shows on Hogmanay, which were to be filmed for broadcast around Europe.

In the audience that night was their producer Steve Lillywhite with his new girlfriend, singer Kirsty MacColl. MacColl would go on to grace the Barrowland stage in her own right, guesting with the Pogues in December 1987 for the live debut of 'Fairytale Of New York'. On this first visit, however, she received – and accepted – a marriage proposal from Lillywhite as a pipe band played in the new year. MacColl's romantic recollection of the experience was that 'it all started with a bang under a starlit sky'.

BLONDIE BRING IN THE BELLS

New York icons Blondie played two seminal gigs at the Apollo, the first in 1977 when they were touring with Television. Guitarist Chris Stein remembers that 'by some quirk of fate, the Ramones and Talking Heads were playing at Strathclyde University. The local media was all about CBGB's in Glasgow'.

Stein's first impression of the Apollo was of a 'cavernous space'. He also noted the infamous high stage saying: 'Fans couldn't rush the stage without siege ladders.'

The band then played two nights in December 1979, the second on Hogmanay. The show was broadcast live on BBC's *The Old Grey Whistle Test* and featured a guest appearance on 'Sunday Girl' by the Strathclyde Police Pipe Band. Drummer Clem Burke had a gold drum kit and decided he wanted stage wear to match, saying, 'I didn't tell anyone, I just showed up with this gold suit that was made for me by Marc Bolan's tailor.'

THE BIG DAY

Subtitled Music from the Heart of Glasgow, The Big Day was the biggest free concert ever staged in Scotland, attracting a quarter of a million fans to four stages around the city on 3 June 1990. It became the shop window of Glasgow's year as European City of Culture, with Channel 4 broadcasting live from the thronging streets.

Forty artists were booked to perform across Glasgow Green, the People's Palace, George Square and the intimate Riverside Stage at Custom House Quay, where an unannounced Michael Stipe popped up to guest with Billy Bragg alongside 10,000 Maniacs singer Natalie Merchant.

An appearance by the Pogues was nixed by police for fear of stoking sectarian tensions while Deacon Blue frontman Ricky Ross spoke up in support of Ravenscraig steelworkers and dedicated their set to the people of Glasgow 'with no homes to go to'. Although the event was free, the organisers encouraged donations for the city's young homeless.

Hometown heroes including Wet Wet Wet, John Martyn, Texas, Love & Money, Hue & Cry, Eddi Reader and the Silencers spread the love and, for one day only, the likes of Big Country, Hothouse Flowers, Average White Band, Nanci Griffith, Hugh Masekela and Dick Gaughan were counted as honorary Glaswegians.

That privilege was not extended to Bellshill diva Sheena Easton, returning to Scotland after hitting the big time in the States via some saucy collaborations with Prince. Addressing her people with a mid-Atlantic accent, she allegedly gushed 'it's great to be back in England' only to be whacked by a glowstick and heckled with quintessentially (and, we have to say, offensive) Glaswegian chants of 'purple dwarf shagger'.

OASIS AT TUT'S

Of all the legendary gigs in Glasgow, the fateful evening in May 1993 when a group of lairy Mancunians bulldozed their way on to the bottom of a four-band bill at a small but mighty venue is the one with the widest ripple effect. As all sixty-nine paying customers at that show – and the thousands more who have claimed they were in attendance – know all too well, this was the night that Oasis were discovered at King Tut's Wah Wah Hut.

Local indie bands 18 Wheeler and Boyfriend were the co-headliners on a Creation Records bill, with Manchester's Sister Lovers booked to open. They arrived with their friends' band in tow, who were expecting Boyfriend to make good on their casual invitation to join the line-up.

A compromise was struck: the gatecrashers would be paid in beers for a pithy four-song set at the start of the night, which only around a dozen souls actually witnessed. Fortunately, one of those souls was Creation boss Alan McGee who knew he had found his next signing. The songs which sealed the deal were 'Rock 'n' Roll Star', 'Bring It On Down', 'Up In The Sky' and 'I Am The Walrus'.

A few years later, the all-conquering Oasis were presented with the original King Tut's sign; Noel Gallagher still keeps it in his London office. Meanwhile, back in the venue where it all started, the urinals in the men's toilets were dubbed the Wonderwall.

HELLO, GLASGOW . . . !

It is a truth universally acknowledged that Glasgow gig audiences are the best in the world. Little wonder that so many artists have recorded live albums in the city, from Bert Jansch's *Young Man Blues* to the Kinks' *Live At Kelvin Hall*, which was heavily overdubbed in order that listeners might discern the band above the crowd hysteria.

The list would be a lot shorter were it not for the storied Apollo. AC/DC and Status Quo both recorded their first live albums at the venue (*If You Want Blood* and the recently reissued *Live!*), with the former returning to the stage in Scotland football strips and the latter handing out stickers saying 'I'm on the Quo album'.

Rush thanked 'the Glaswegian chorus' for their backing vocal contribution to *Exit Stage Left*, partly recorded at the Apollo, while the Ramones cut to the chase on *It's Alive* and used the crowd noise from their December 1977 show to enhance the gig recording from London's Rainbow Theatre.

In contrast, Frightened Rabbit recorded an acoustic set in the tiny Captain's Rest basement and released it in 2009 as *Quietly Now!*

BOWIE AT THE BARRAS

David Bowie playing in your backyard is always a special occasion. The Thin White Duke has graced Glasgow with his presence on many occasions, but there was a special frisson when he played the blessed Barrowland on 22 July 1997. Although promoting his drum 'n' bass-inspired album *Earthling*, he thrilled the capacity crowd by opening the set with a solo acoustic version of 'Quicksand' and cherry-picking classics such as 'Fame', 'Fashion' and 'The Jean Genie' from his back catalogue.

This was not, however, Bowie's first appearance at the hallowed East End ballroom. He had played with his lesser-loved band Tin Machine in 1991 when it was alleged that one of the stars studded into Barrowland's iconic curved ceiling had fallen on to the Starman during the quakingly loud soundcheck. In truth, one of the venue crew had dislodged one to present to Bowie, who prized his Barrowland star enough to frame and hang it above the toilet door in his Paris abode.

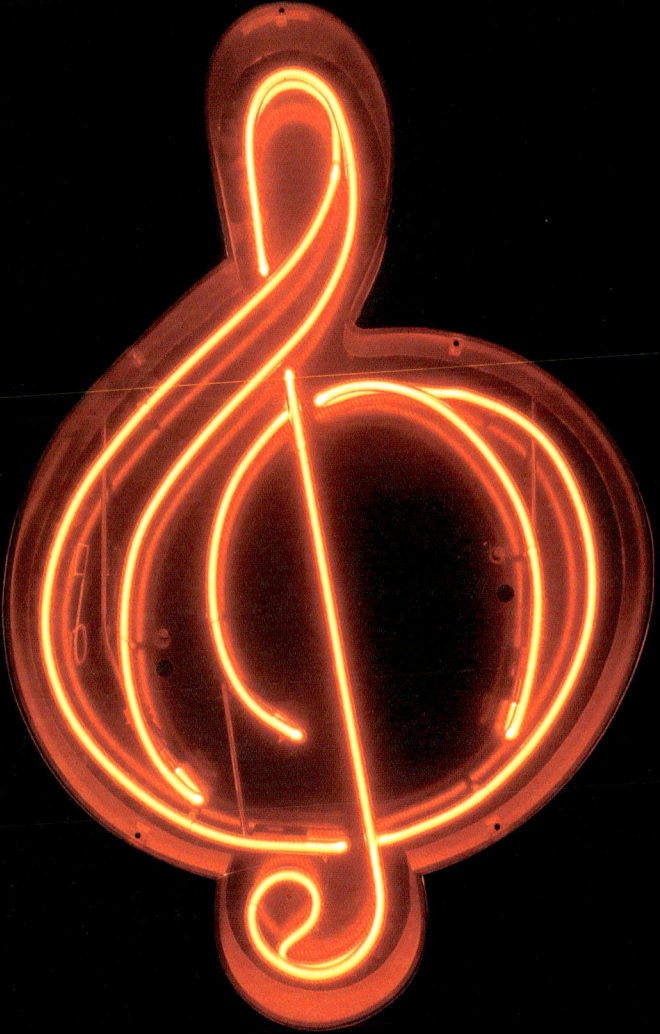

BARROWLAND/ BARROWLAND PARK

As venues go, Barrowland is the toppermost of the poppermost. Don't take our word for it – Oasis and Metallica both hail this family-owned ballroom in the East End as the world's greatest gig. It has inspired songs by Christy Moore, Amy MacDonald and Simple Minds, who played a key role in Barrowland's revival when in 1983 they used it as the location for their monumental 'Waterfront' video.

Prior to its rebirth as a concert venue, Barrowland had already clocked up almost fifty years as a ballroom. Opening in 1934 as the Barrowland Palais de Danse above the stalls of the Barras market, it was conceived by owner Margaret McIver as a space for her workers to relax after a hard day's hawking and take a birl around the floor to the strains of house band Billy McGregor & the Gaybirds.

Its original rooftop sign of a trader pushing a 'barra' was quite the flashy landmark. During the Second World War, Nazi propaganda broadcaster Lord Haw Haw even suggested that German fighter pilots might navigate by the sign, which was then swiftly removed for the remainder of the conflict. When the original Barrowland was gutted by fire in 1958, all that was salvaged was the cartwheel from the sign. It now hangs from the foyer ceiling of the 'new' Barrowland, opened in 1960 with its famous Canadian maple sprung dancefloor and barrel-shaped ceiling.

In the 60s, Barrowland was graced with visiting jazz and rock 'n' roll greats, including the Rolling Stones, who pocketed a £5 fee for their appearance in January 1964. The venue was also frequented by local razor gangs, each with rigid territorial boundaries around the dancefloor. Most infamously, and awfully, three women were murdered in 1968 and 1969 by the serial killer dubbed 'Bible John' after attending the dancehall.

The ballroom's heyday had long passed by the time Simple Minds kick-started its rebirth as a gig venue in November 1983, but it quickly became a roaring favourite with fans and bands.

The venue certainly made an impression on Bob Dylan when he played on 24 June 2004, breaking tradition to shimmy, smile and – heaven forfend – actually speak to the audience. Following a lusty singalong to 'Like a Rolling Stone', Dylan was moved to comment that 'we musta played that song a thousand times, and no one's ever kept up like that . . .'

Stone Roses guitarist John Squire's impressions of Barrowland are all tied up with the smell wafting from the venue's hot dog stall. There would be no frying tonight whenever noted vegetarian Chrissie Hynde played with the Pretenders, but the sausage stand has long gone to make way for a bijou unit selling Barrowland merchandise emblazoned with their iconic logo. The huge Barrowland sign with its happy lettering surrounded by shooting stars is a neon masterpiece and the celestial theme pervades the building. David Bowie caught his own Barrowland star (see page 79), and visiting performers regularly prise a star from the dressing-room walls. Scott Hutchison, late frontman of heart-on-sleeve indie rockers Frightened Rabbit, used to mount his on top of his Christmas tree.

The Barrowland Hall of Fame has honoured legends onstage and behind the scenes since 2015, while just along the Gallowgate in Barrowland Park, the Album Pathway namechecks the 664 headliners who had played up until the memorial was laid in late 2013. The multicoloured concrete strips commemorating individual gigs were designed by artist and onetime musician Jim Lambie to emulate the look of record spines on a shelf. A walk along the Pathway captures a legion of fond memories this hallowed hall has thrown up over forty years of glorious gigging.

Allow us to share one more: Manchester's mighty New Order were a strictly encore-free zone in the mid-80s but when they played Barrowland on 16 February 1985, fans filing out of the venue after the main set were wrongfooted when the group returned to the stage to play again, with bassist Peter Hook crowing, 'Fooled you!' When asked afterwards why they had chosen to perform an encore in Glasgow that night, the band replied, 'Because we were told we would get our heads kicked in if we didn't.'

THE SCOTIA

The Scotia Bar on Stockwell Street *claims* to be the oldest pub in Glasgow, but you'll get no argument from us that this cosy L-shaped bar is undoubtedly one of the liveliest and most atmospheric hostelries in the city. Replete with low ceilings, wooden panelling, fireplace and snug, it has always been conducive to a live music session and, by the mid-60s, the Scotia was the hub of Glasgow's folk scene, welcoming international visitors such as Tom Paxton and the Dubliners as well as local rockers the Poets and members of the future Sensational Alex Harvey Band.

The Scotia's most famous son is comedian, consummate banjo picker and all-round national hero Billy Connolly, who presided over the pub singarounds in the early 70s and performed regularly with his pals Tam Harvey, then Gerry Rafferty, as the Humblebums (see page 13).

Local laws allowed for singing only in the lounge area of pubs, so the sessions took place in what was dubbed the Wee Back Room, scene of much scrutiny by the local constabulary, who succeeded in shutting down the singarounds for a time. The musicians responded with a picket line and temporary boycott. All this despite the presence on the other side of the pub of local motorcycle gang, the Blue Angels. Generally, these twain never met although, occasionally, one of the Angels would cross the tracks and play his banjo at the session before returning to the dark side to restore the tribal harmony.

Described by Sir Winston Churchill as 'Scotland's greatest ever ambassador', Harry Lauder launched his career at the Britannia Panopticon.

A Britannia poster from 1896 (bought on eBay from a man in Arizona!).

Matilda Alice Powles (stage name Vesta Tilley) became England's highest-earning woman in the 1890s.

The Scotia forms a trad pub triumvirate with the Clutha and Victoria bars on the Clydeside and, to this day, remains the place to go for a mix of live music residencies and lively political and cultural commentary from the regulars, some of whom have been drinking – and possibly singing – there since the 60s.

BRITANNIA PANOPTICON

Tucked away on a nondescript lane off Glasgow's busy Argyle Street, you'll find the entrance to the Britannia Panopticon, the world's oldest surviving music hall.

The building first opened in 1779 as a warehouse and was to be converted into a department store until the architect realised that a music hall was more appropriate to the needs of the locals.

This hidden gem first opened as the 1,500-capacity Britannia Vaults in 1857 and survived for the next eighty-one years when other music halls burned down. With no toilet facilities to speak of, audience members urinated where they stood, rendering this wooden building both fire- and woodworm-retardant.

Its most enterprising manager A.E. Pickard, Yorkshire's answer to P.T. Barnum, took over in 1906 and turned the premises into Glasgow's first entertainment multiplex with a cinema, indoor zoo, waxworks and freakshow all under one roof.

The great Scottish music hall star Sir Harry Lauder performed one of his first professional gigs in the Panopticon, while young acrobat Archie Leach appeared with the Bob Pender troupe before finding Hollywood fame as Cary Grant. In 1906, a sixteen-year-old Stan Laurel made his stage debut here but fluffed his turn so badly that he unwittingly discovered a talent for slapstick.

Pickard closed the Panopticon in 1938 and it lay dormant for almost sixty years before its revival as a modern music hall by staff and volunteers committed to conserving this treasured piece of entertainment history.

THE GLASGOW ATHENAEUM/ROYAL CONSERVATOIRE OF SCOTLAND

The Royal Conservatoire of Scotland is arguably the most musically influential institution in the country – in fact, it regularly features in the top rankings for performing arts schools around the world. Its School of Music has been bolstered in the last few decades by the Alexander Gibson

Opera School and courses in traditional music, bagpiping and jazz, and Glasgow is hugely enriched by the budding talents of its three thousand students, spilling out into venues, sessions and festivals across the city.

The Conservatoire was originally founded as the Glasgow Athenaeum in 1847, with Charles Dickens hailing it as 'an educational example and encouragement to the rest of Scotland' at its inaugural banquet. Austrian-born Emma Ritter-Bondy was appointed Professor of Piano in 1892, making her the first female professor in the UK.

Cecil Williams, who became principal of the then Royal Scottish Academy of Music and Drama in 1965, had been an anti-apartheid campaigner in South Africa and was instrumental in securing Nelson Mandela the freedom of the city of Glasgow in 1981. Renaming the RSAMD's St George's Place address as Nelson Mandela Place was all the sweeter because the South African consulate was also located there.

Esteemed Conservatoire alumni include Alan Cumming, Ruby Wax, James McAvoy, *Outlander* star Sam Heughan, opera singer Karen Cargill and the *Doctor Who* double of David Tennant and Ncuti Gatwa, while its most famous dropout is surely Jack Bruce. The late Cream bassist was known in his day for spending as much time in the city's post-war jazz dives as at his studies, but is now honoured by his sometime alma mater with a memorial sculpture incorporating his bass strings and inscribed with his adage that 'failure can be a triumph, but fear of failure is always a disaster'.

KING TUT'S WAH WAH HUT
Even if Oasis had failed to blag their way on to a bill way back in 1993, King Tut's Wah Wah Hut would still be the most celebrated small venue in Glasgow. Its most famous piece of pop lore is recounted elsewhere in this book (see page 77), leaving room here to hail some of the many other memorable snapshots in its 35-year history.

The wee venue with the big reputation opened in February 1990 on the former site of dive bar Saints & Sinners with the aspiration to scrub up the scuzzy reputation of the nation's 'toilet circuit' of grassroots venues. Very quickly it gained accolades as Radio 1's Best UK Live Venue – and plaudits for its mushroom soup from the Manic Street Preachers who played the venue three times in 1991, ticket sales inching up with each appearance.

Tut's has long functioned as the first rung of the touring ladder for artists making their debut appearance in the city, be they complete unknowns such as Blur, who played to forty people in the summer of 1990, future stadium fillers Coldplay and Muse, pop prospects from Paloma Faith to Olivia Dean, or your new favourite bands Suede, the Strokes and Arctic Monkeys, each surfing the crest of a huge hype wave in 1992, 2001 and 2005 respectively.

As for bragging rights, perhaps you were in the room when the world's future highest paid DJ Calvin Harris made his first ever live appearance in December 2006, or when KT Tunstall stepped up to play

King Tut's took its memorable name from a New York club and theatre space.

2014 BENJAMIN BOOKER, SAINT RAYMOND,

2013 DISCLOSURE, THE 1975, TOM ODELL, THE TWILIGHT SAD, CLEAN BANDIT,

2012... ALABAMA SHAKES, JAKE BUGG, PALMA VIOLETS, GABRIELLE APLIN, THE 1975, TWIN ATLANTIC

2011... TRIBES, THE VIEW, MILES KANE, BEN HOWARD, BIG COUNTRY, METRONOMY, RIVAL SONS

2010... PAOLO NUTINI, MANIC STREET PREACHERS, ELLIE GOULDING, EVERYTHING EVERYTHING, TWO DOOR CINEMA CLUB, DARWIN DEEZ

2009... THE BREEDERS, PALOMA FAITH, THE TEMPER TRAP, LITTLE BOOTS, LA ROUX, MUMFORD & SONS

2008... FLORENCE AND THE MACHINE, THE TING TINGS, WHITE LIES, THE SCRIPT, FRIENDLY FIRES, YOU ME AT SIX, DUFFY

2007... GLASVEGAS, THE ENEMY, AMY MACDONALD, JACK PENATE, CALVIN HARRIS, NEWTON FAULKNE, OCEAN COLOUR SCENE

keyboards and recorder for her buddy Half Cousin on the very night that her star-making TV debut on *Later with Jools Holland* was broadcast to the nation. Maybe you saw Biffy Clyro on at least one or two of the dozen occasions they played the venue on their slowburn ascent to become the biggest rock band in Scotland, maybe you are twisting the truth a little when you claim that you were one of the cool dozen who witnessed that legendary Oasis set – or maybe you are liking the sound of the bright young things playing next week . . .

SUB CLUB

If it's Saturday night on Jamaica Street, it must be Subculture at the Sub Club with Harri and Domenic on the decks. The world's longest running weekly house and techno night is a talisman for this legendary basement club, upholding its ethos to favour resident DJs over bigger name guests, to keep it intimate rather than expand to larger premises.

In a previous life, the Sub Club, or the Subbie to its loyal patrons, was after-hours speakeasy Le Cavé, hosting late-night jams with visiting jazz greats Louis Armstrong and Ella Fitzgerald. In the 70s, the Jamaica Inn hosted disco dinner dances with DJ Dougie Donnelly, of later sports broadcasting renown, and Primal Scream played one of their first gigs in its incarnation as Lucifers nightclub.

The Sub Club opened on 1 April 1987 – no joke as, within a year, acid house had transformed the clubbing landscape and this 400-capacity room had found (one of) its tribes. Its early days are inextricably linked with techno titans Stuart McMillian and Orde Meikle, aka Slam, who helmed Joy on Fridays and then Atlantis on Saturdays before moving to the Arches.

James 'Harri' Harrigan and Domenic Capello took over Saturdays in 1994 and have been rocking the house ever since – despite an agonising three-year closure at the turn of the millennium following a fire in neighbouring premises. Trailblazing Chicago house DJs Derrick Carter and Mr Fingers himself, Larry Heard, have guested at the Subbie but when the singular Optimo reigned Sunday nights, DJs JD Twitch and JG Wilkes ruled the booth themselves and booked live acts instead, from Franz Ferdinand to LCD Soundsystem to Lee 'Scratch' Perry.

The Numbers club and label spawned the next wave of homegrown electronica talent. Rustie, Hudson Mohawke (who used to collect the glasses at the club) and the late SOPHIE went on to work respectively with rapper Danny Brown, Kanye West and Lady Gaga. As to the next generation, Harri's son Jasper James has joined the Subculture squad, so get on the vibrating bodysonic dancefloor and feel that bass.

CIVIC GEMS

Glasgow's civic concert venues play a significant role in the city's cultural life, not least as the homes of two of Scotland's national orchestras, the Royal Scottish National Orchestra and the BBC Scottish Symphony Orchestra.

The RSNO's roots go back to 1843 when an orchestra was established to accompany the Glasgow Choral Union – the RSNO Chorus as they are today. In its time, the orchestra has been based in Saint Andrew's Halls (see page 34) and the Henry Wood Hall but took up residence in the **Royal Concert Hall** which has loomed over Buchanan Street since 1990, welcoming visiting orchestras and conductors, rock and pop, soul and country luminaries from Johnny Cash to Al Green and the folk hordes who bring the buzz to its 2,500-capacity auditorium during annual winter hoolie Celtic Connections (see page 113).

Merchant City jewel the **City Halls** is Glasgow's longest-serving entertainment venue, opened in 1841 and immediately hailed for its fine acoustic. This acoustic was used to great effect by abolitionist and orator Frederick Douglass, whose 1846 visit to the city inspired the folk song 'Send Back The Money' (see page 101).

The Scottish Chamber Orchestra played their first ever concert here in 1974 and continue to programme spring and autumn seasons, alongside the BBC SSO, who made the City Halls their base following refurbishment of the building in 2006.

Sister venue the **Old Fruitmarket** lay dormant for many years when the market moved to new premises, but this characterful space was salvaged for the city by the Glasgow Jazz Festival (see page 112), who hosted its first concert, the Jools Holland Big Band, in 1993. Annie Ross wasn't the only songbird in the room the following year when her set was disrupted by a chorus of blackbirds in the rafters, while Lunasa's Celtic Connections show was interrupted by the triggering of the fire alarm. The 1,500-capacity audience were duly ejected on to Candleriggs,

The Royal Concert Hall: a Buchanan Street landmark since 1990.

where a local resident kept the tunes flowing by blasting Irish rebel songs from his second-floor sound system.

KELVINGROVE BANDSTAND

With its bijou stage, intimate terrace-style seating, atmospheric lighting and open-air riverside setting, the Kelvingrove Bandstand is one of Glasgow's prettiest and best-loved venues, fêted by patrons and performers alike.

Music legends Patti Smith, Burt Bacharach, Brian Wilson and Siouxsie Sioux have all played the annual Summer Nights at the Bandstand, a concert series so good-natured that Van Morrison almost cracked a smile at his appearance in 2022. Nile Rodgers hailed Chic's two Bandstand concerts in 2017 – one rain, one shine – as 'unforgettable. The enthusiasm and decibel level of the crowd was insane.'

The Kelvingrove Bandstand and Amphitheatre, to give its full civic title, was built in 1924, hosting a diverse programme of classical and jazz concerts, military bands, ballroom dances, Poll Tax protests, punk picnics and Radio Clyde's free festivals until it fell into disrepair in the 90s.

But this cherished Category B listed structure is the last remaining bandstand in the city and its denizens refused to let it crumble. Teenage Fanclub and Belle and Sebastian, who had both filmed music videos there in its wilderness years, were among the artists campaigning for its renovation. Both played when it re-opened in summer 2014, with Belle and Sebastian doing the honours to mark the opening ceremony of the Commonwealth Games, bouncing onstage in matching maroon tracksuits, dancing with thistle mascot Clyde and, naturally, performing 'The Stars of Track and Field'.

HYDRO/ARMADILLO

Sitting on the in-filled Queen's Dock, the Scottish Event Campus is not the most snappily named of Glasgow's many celebrated venues. However, the SEC, which comprises the SEC Centre, the Armadillo and the Hydro, has hosted some of the city's most popular gigs since UB40 played the first concert at the Clydeside complex in 1985.

Designed by Foster + Partners and completed in 1997, the Clyde Auditorium added a further 3,000-capacity venue to the original SEC site and eventually adopted its Armadillo nickname as its official designation. Acts as diverse as Grace Jones, Leonard Cohen, Susan Boyle and

THE OVO HYDRO

Motörhead plus the unusual double bill of Status Quo and Shakin' Stevens have all graced the Armadillo stage.

As vital as the existing campus had been in redeveloping the docklands area, arguably the real game-changer was the launch of the 14,300-capacity Hydro in 2013, attracting superstars from Madonna to The Who, from the Killers to Dolly Parton to its state-of-the-art amphitheatre. The façade glowed purple for Prince in 2014, Beyoncé used the venue as her rehearsal studio for the Mrs. Carter Show World Tour and the Hydro was a key location for the 2020 film *Eurovision Song Contest: The Story of Fire Saga*, meaning Glasgow can now boast that it has – sort of – hosted the Eurovision Song Contest.

THE GARAGE

If you are walking west along Sauchiehall Street, you can't really miss the Garage with its yellow lorry logo sticking out over the entrance. Behind its doors and up its staircase – lined with the names of artists who have graced its stage over the years – lies a club which has trucked through the decades in several different incarnations, first as the Gainsborough and Astoria ballrooms, then as dedicated rock venue the Electric Garden, hosting shows by the likes of Pink Floyd, Slade and Deep Purple, before housing Shuffles nightclub in the 70s and the Mayfair venue in the 80s.

This 700-capacity hall re-opened as the Garage in 1994, booking early gigs by Coldplay, One Direction and shock rocker Marilyn Manson, whose show was picketed by local fire and brimstone preacher Pastor Jack Glass. Its sister rock club The Cathouse hosted an early appearance in Glasgow by Oasis, but the Garage wins the most prestigious guest award for welcoming Prince and his band on 15 March 1995. Earlier that evening, the Minneapolis maestro had played to 10,000 fans at the SEC – most of whom would later claim to have attended the Garage aftershow concert too. Prince made the crowd wait before rocking the house at 2 a.m., then sashaying down the venue

stairs and (allegedly) doing a forward roll into his waiting limousine – coloured purple, of course.

THIRD EYE CENTRE/CCA

The Centre for Contemporary Arts (CCA) on Sauchiehall Street does what it says on the tin. It's an exhibition space, a gig venue, a café/bar, a cinema and a performance space all under one roof.

In a previous life it was known as the Third Eye Centre, founded in 1974 by the writer and playwright Tom McGrath. Described by the *Guardian* as 'a shrine to the avant-garde', it hosted visiting artists and performers such as Allen Ginsberg, Whoopi Goldberg, John Byrne, Damien Hirst and Edwin Morgan, quickly gaining a reputation as the focus for Glasgow's counterculture. Notable guests also included Billy Connolly, who played at the opening of a John Byrne exhibition, and Ivor Cutler who recorded his *Life In A Scotch Sitting Room, Vol.2* album live in July 1977.

The building re-opened as the CCA in 1992 and carried on the legacy as a hub and hangout. After a major refurbishment in 2001, the new space opened to the public with a party which included a DJ set by Jarvis Cocker, live music from notorious New York duo Suicide and a new commission by multi-media art-house and production company Cryptic.

SAINT LUKE'S

Saint Luke's & the Winged Ox is a thriving multipurpose music venue, bar and restaurant. The converted church in Bain Street is a stone's throw from Barrowland and hard to miss with its striking mural of a winged ox (the beast being the symbol of the original Saint Luke) by renowned street artist, Smug.

The former Saint Luke's and Saint Andrew's parish church had lain vacant since 2012 when local brothers Michael and Tony Woods decided to buy it. Their hunch, that the space could be converted to a great music venue, proved correct. Saint Luke's famed acoustics has made it the go-to venue for intimate acoustic gigs. The original pipe organ is a fitting backdrop, the wraparound balcony is made for podium queens and its wooden pulpit conveniently serves as a DJ booth.

Gerry Cinnamon and Lewis Capaldi played sold-out gigs in the same month in 2017. Capaldi handed out three disposable cameras to the

The winged ox is the symbol of the original Saint Luke.

700-capacity crowd and was amazed that all were returned, but expressed his disappointment that every photograph was family friendly, saying: 'Glasgow, I thought better of you.'

KEEPING IT LOCAL

Any healthy music culture grows from the ground upwards and in Glasgow the grassroots scene is lovingly fed and watered by an impressive array of committed small venues which foster a sense of community among their regulars.

Nice N Sleazy is the daddy of the scene, opened on Sauchiehall Street in the grungy early 90s with a CBGB scuzziness to the décor and a basement venue which hosted early shows by Franz Ferdinand, Mogwai and the Twilight Sad. Snow Patrol's Gary Lightbody spent so much time propping up the bar when he lived in Glasgow that it was assumed he was staff. Like the Ramones, it got everything right from the start, so why change?

Meanwhile over on Bath Street, the bold **Bloc+** has forged its own free and free-thinking underground music programme. The neon sign says 'not for everyone', but it is well worth testing those limits.

Sister venues **Mono** and **Stereo** wear their indie destination reputation with cool, casual style and a side order of vegan food. This is where Glasgow's alternative arts community comes to play and plot. Across the lane from Stereo, **Old Hairdressers** is the ultimate in shabby chic. Its upstairs venue promotes a melting pot of experimental music, art, theatre and filmmaking.

In the West End, the **Hug & Pint** established its credentials by referencing an Arab Strap album in its name. Its basement venue may be snug, but its music policy is broad. Over on the Southside, the **Glad Café** and the **Rum Shack** are both relaxed and eclectic hangouts, the former boasting a tip-top line-up of indie, folk and jazz, the latter pulsing with its roots and groove-orientated clubs.

If you want to get to the heart of Glasgow's musical matter, hang out in any one, or preferably all, of these vital venues. We think you'll find they are for everyone.

STUDENT UNIONS

Student Unions played a crucial role in Glasgow's music scene at a time when live venues in the city were few and far between.

The Rhythm Divine: bringing good vibes to Glasgow's dance floors since 1990.

Strathclyde University's Student Union on John Street has hosted an impressive gig roster including The Who, Elton John, Fleetwood Mac, Pink Floyd, the Kinks and The Jam. In 1977 the Ramones, with Talking Heads as support, nearly didn't play when the Lord Provost declared: 'Glasgow has enough yobs of its own . . . We don't need to import them.'

Over at Glasgow University, the **Queen Margaret Union/QM** was the chosen venue for early gigs by Queen, the Smiths, Coldplay and, most notably, Nirvana's only Glasgow show on 30 November 1991. Such was the I-was-there kudos that Dave Grohl's handwritten (in black marker pen capitals) set list sold at auction for £5,625 in 2014.

In the late 80s, the city's goths converged on the Glasgow Tech disco but, from 1990, the Vic bar at **Glasgow School of Art** became the alternative hangout for local musicians and artists when DJ Andrew Symington started his influential club, Divine. His audacious mix of musical styles influenced Optimo's JD Twitch, and visiting musicians including Evan Dando, Jack White, Courtney Love and Pete Shelley all paid homage on the dancefloor.

In his tireless fight against slavery, special reformer Frederick Douglass toured Scotland many times between 1846 and 1860, delivering impassioned lectures to standing-room-only audiences. He visited Robert Burns' sister in Ayr and frequently quoted the poet's work in his meetings. While in Glasgow in 1846, he resided as a guest in the Gallowgate home of Quaker grocer William Smeal.

DID YOU KNOW?

SLAVES' LAMENTS AND WHISTLIN' KIRKS

When the renowned abolitionist and writer Frederick Douglass came to speak at the City Halls in 1846, he was surely aware of Glasgow's commercial links to the transatlantic slave trade. He spoke out particularly against the slaveholder donations accepted by the Free Church of Scotland and his (ultimately unsuccessful) campaign to 'send back the money' inspired a protest song of the same name which condemned the 'dark, polluted gold'.

Douglass was a great admirer of Robert Burns, who had changed his plans to find work on a slave plantation and written his own anti-slavery song, 'The Slave's Lament', more than fifty years earlier. When in Glasgow, Burns would sup and stay at the Black Bull Inn on Argyle Street where he composed his clandestine love letters to Agnes McElhose, the married woman who inspired his immortal love song 'Ae Fond Kiss'.

Agnes was married close to her Saltmarket roots in Saint Andrew's in the Square, the magnificent neoclassical church around which Saint Andrew's Square was laid – but not before renowned Italian aeronaut Vincenzo Lunardi had launched a hot-air balloon from the site and given his name to the fashionable puffy bonnet namechecked by Burns in 'To A Louse'.

Saint Andrew's in the Square became a much-loved if underused venue from the turn of the millennium, but back in the early nineteenth century its relationship with live music was more contentious as the installation of a harmonium organ to accompany worship stoked 'a controversy of a prolonged and bitter character' across the city. The Glasgow Presbytery took a dim view of such fripperies – much to the chagrin of the church's rather more receptive congregation.

Perhaps they felt left out as their neighbours at Saint Andrew's by the Green had warmly welcomed their church organ, the first in the city. Indeed, they were so enthusiastic that they were dubbed the 'Whistlin' Kirk'.

GOING UP THE CLYDE

Folk icon Woody Guthrie is best known for his socialist anthem 'This Land Is Your Land' but during the Second World War, while he was serving in the US Merchant Navy, this city was briefly his city as he spent a few days of shore leave drinking and playing his way up and down the hostelries of the Clydeside with fellow singer-songwriter seaman Cisco Houston, while they waited for their ship to be repaired. The Victoria Bar and the long-gone Betty's Bar on Lancefield Quay are among those claiming that 'Guthrie Gigged Here'.

Glasgow left an impression on the father of protest music and he wrote a set of lyrics about the city as he sailed home along the Clyde, bidding farewell to the landscape, the people and their politics. Sixty years later, his daughter Nora discovered 'Scotch Hills', alternatively known as 'Going Up the Clyde', in her father's notebooks and passed the words to Billy Bragg who added his own music and performed Guthrie's Glasgow paean in the city which captured his imagination and, reportedly, emptied his wallet.

GLASGOW BANS PUNK

Blame it on the Sex Pistols. If they hadn't used naughty words on the primetime *Today* show, their gig at Glasgow's Apollo may not have been pulled, the city fathers may not have noticed that the visiting Ramones were singing about sniffing glue in a town blighted by solvent abuse and a delegation of councillors may never have attended the Stranglers' gig at the City Halls on 22 June 1977 to witness an incidence of what one described as 'highly disturbing' 'induced hysteria'. Or a stage invasion, as more seasoned concertgoers might call it.

The City Halls 'riot' resulted in an unofficial (and unenforceable) ban on punk rock in Glasgow. Most of the city's small clubs and hostelries were not minded to test the limits of the council's tolerance, but there remained a handful of rebel establishments where fans could get their limited punk kicks. The Mars Bar, situated just off St Enoch Square, offered a weekly residency to one of the city's few punk outfits,

Johnny & the Self-Abusers, just as they were trying out a new band name: Simple Minds.

Glasgow's loss was Paisley's gain with fans bused from Bruce's Records on Union Street beyond the city limits to the punk-friendly Bungalow Bar on Renfrew Road and the Silver Thread Hotel on Blackhall Street, where the enterprising Disco Harry promoted mid-week New Wave Nights and a character called Kenny Clash would charge £1 for a safety pin piercing of the mouth.

Inspired by the likes of Generation X, Elvis Costello, the Rezillos, the Adverts and the Boomtown Rats playing in their own town, Paisley's homegrown punk scene flourished. The 1979 Ferguslie Park Festival took place on 23 June 1979 with a bill including local bands the Fegs, named after their Ferguslie 'hood, and Defiant Pose, featuring actor David Tennant's brother Blair McDonald on drums before he relocated to London and became a big shot in music publishing.

Addressing allegations of a heavy-handed police presence on the day, a spokesperson for Strathclyde Police said, 'I totally refute the claim that there were thirty officers in attendance.' Paisley independent label Groucho Marxist Records responded by releasing the punk compilation EP *Ha! Ha! Funny Polis*.

UP THE WORKERS

The great trade unionist Jimmy Reid said during the historic Upper Clyde Shipbuilders' work-in of 1971 to 1972, that 'folk music has no meaning unless it expresses the lives and struggles of ordinary people' and the folk musicians of Glasgow and beyond stepped up in solidarity, recording an album *Unity Creates Strength* to support the strike fund. Danny Kyle, Dominic Behan, Robin Hall and Jimmie MacGregor were among the artists who gave their services for free.

Donovan headlined a UCS benefit concert at Green's Playhouse for the workers, sharing the bill with artists including Billy Connolly and Gallagher and Lyle. John Lennon and Yoko Ono supported the cause, sending a card which read 'power to the people, with love from John and Yoko', a donation – accounts vary from £500 to £5,000 – and a bunch of red roses, which was passed to the maternity ward at the Southern General Hospital. When word of Lennon's donation spread a wag responded, 'Don't be daft – Lenin's been deid for years.'

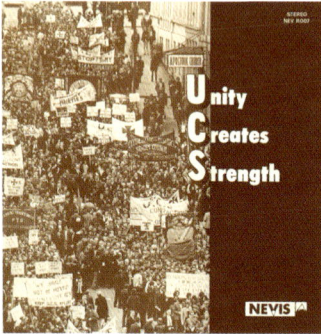

Album producer Jim McLean approached Sean Connery to write the sleeve notes but Sean couldn't meet the deadline. By fortuitous coincidence the LP number was NEVR 007.

The renowned American singer, actor and activist Paul Robeson visited Glasgow in 1960, leading the May Day Parade for International Workers' Day from George Square to Queen's Park, where thousands awaited his arrival. It was reported that you could hear a pin drop when he took to the stage to sing 'Ol' Man River'.

In 2023, Glasgow group the Tenementals – who recount Glasgow's radical history through song – were inspired by a song Robeson had covered. 'Die Moorsoldaten' – or 'The Peat Bog Soldiers' – is a ninety-year-old protest song written by Communist prisoners held in a Nazi concentration camp. The Tenementals' version is now housed in the archives of the Documentation and Information Centre of the Emsland Camps, a few kilometres from the site in north-western Germany where the song was first performed.

DOCTOR WHO AND THE LATE-NIGHT REVOLUTIONARY

Everybody knows you go to art school to form a band and rangy young Bowie freak Peter Capaldi was not inclined to break that tradition during his time at Glasgow School of Art, forming post-punk hopefuls the Dreamboys with teen drummer Craig Ferguson.

Not to be confused with the male striptease troupe of the same name, these Dreamboys were unknown for such non-hits as 'Bela Lugosi's Birthday', with Capaldi lamenting that they were the only band among their Glasgow peers not invited to record a session for the John Peel show.

Ferguson went on to acclaim and fame as shouty comedian Bing Hitler and host of US talk show *The Late Late Show*, while Capaldi achieved national treasure status portraying even shoutier spin doctor

Malcolm Tucker in merciless satire *The Thick of It* and the guitar-slinging twelfth incarnation of *Doctor Who*. Even now, Capaldi evidently still craves some rock stardust, releasing in early 2025 his second solo album, *Sweet Illusions*, on Last Night From Glasgow Records.

VAL D'ORO

A chippie may seem a strange choice for inclusion in a tome on Glasgow music legends but Val D'Oro by Glasgow Cross has many a musical footnote in its salt 'n' vinegar-scented history since it first began trading in 1875. Its tuneful customers include Paul McCartney, Jimmy Logan, Marti Pellow and Teenage Fanclub. Regrettably not all on the same night.

Arguably the biggest legend in his own lunchtime was the recently retired Luigi Corvi. He trained at the RSAMD, now the Royal Conservatoire, but gave up the chance of a singing career to take over the family business. Luigi performed in many venues, including Parkhead where he would regularly belt out arias to footie fans before the match. He also sang in front of Queen Elizabeth II at the 2011 opening of the Scottish Parliament.

But his most regular venue was his chippie, where he would happily give you a song with your supper. While he waited for the police to arrive, Luigi was not averse to sitting on customers who tried to get away without paying for their deep-fried delights.

AXE-WIELDING AT THE APOLLO

The beloved Glasgow Apollo – lionised elsewhere in this book – was a venue with a lively reputation. Marillion frontman Fish affectionately described it a 'warzone'. At least, we think he was being affectionate. The Clash – and their provocative support band – were to find out just how combative when they played there in July 1978.

The venue bouncers gave up on frisking the audience – every second fan was sporting razorblade jewellery. Instead, they got hands on with the crowd during the concert. The febrile atmosphere was later captured in Clash rockumentary *Rude Boy* with Joe Strummer ironically attempting to pacify proceedings before singing 'White Riot'.

Strummer and bassist Paul Simonon were later cuffed and carted off in a police car as the aggro spilled outside. In attendance, a teenage Bobby Gillespie ran home to tell his no-nonsense socialist mammy, who promptly phoned police headquarters demanding they 'Free The Clash now!'

Support band Suicide were used to being bottled. In fact, this New York electro punk duo welcomed it, with frontman Alan Vega often drinking from the proffered vessels. What he was not expecting among the hail of missiles from a riled Apollo audience was an axe, which he later claimed missed him by a whisker. He lived to tell this tall tale but, for one night only, Suicide were very nearly Homicide.

BLUR

invited

fter Show Party

AT

ARCHAOS
V.I.P. Room

EFF BUCKLEY

RIDE

SHAMEN

U2 CONCERT
BY REGULAR MUSIC
FESTIVALS LTD.

BLOCK X

£10.00

INCLUDING BOOKING FEE PLUS VA

STANDING

Nº 3458

rs. July 30 at 7.30 p

Doors open 6.30 p.m

R BY DOOR 4.1 WEST END OF HA

VIDEOS OR RECORDING EQUIPM

KING T

Artist:

Date:

Price:

THIRD EYE CENTRE
IRN BRU ROX WEEK
CAPTAIN AMERICA
EWEARER OVER 18'S O

OVEMBER

: £3.50

oking fee

Straight Jacket Fits

DINOSAURJNR
+ SUPPORT

PM-2AM

ALEX CHI
with Teenage F

BELLE AND SEBASTIAN

ay 8th april doo
13th note, glass

EASTIE BOYS

The Arches
253 Argyle Street, Glasg

Wednesday 28th Februa
Doors 7:30pm
Tickets £9.00 In Advance

OVER 18's ONLY
Please Bring Proof Of Age

SECC
GLASGOW

KENNEDY STREET ENTERPRISES
present

take that

plus guests

EDNESDAY 1st DECEMBER 1993

DOORS 6.30pm   SHOWTIME 7.30pm

adiohead

LAST NIGHT FROM GLASGOW

THE ECOSYSTEM

RECORD LABELS

Postcard Records may have lit the indie fires back at the turn of the 80s, but there has been no shortage of Glasgow-based independent record labels to carry the flame onwards.

The Delgados founded **Chemikal Underground** in 1994 at a time when independently released records could still sell handsomely. They enjoyed a purple patch with a roster including Bis, Arab Strap and Mogwai and continue to keep the faith with releases by Broken Chanter and Chrysanths, with the latter's poised, idiosyncratic debut album *Leave No Shadow* released in September 2024.

Mogwai set up their own **Rock Action Records** in 1995, helming some of the most acclaimed albums to come out of Glasgow and beyond by the Scottish Album of the Year Award-winning likes of Kathryn Joseph and Sacred Paws. **Creeping Bent** has maintained a flow of cool left-of-centre music over the past thirty years by a mix of local talent and cult punk veterans such as The Pop Group's Gareth Sager and Subway Sect's dapper frontman Vic Godard but has elected to wrap up operations at the end of 2025.

Electric Honey, run by the Music Business course at Kelvin College (originally at Stow College), has been described as the most successful student-run label in the world. They took a chance on an ambitious new group called Belle and Sebastian in 1996, releasing their limited edition and thus extremely collectable debut album *Tigermilk* and doubling down with 'Starfighter Pilot', the debut single by Snow Patrol (going under their previous name Polarbear), and then Biffy Clyro's debut EP *thekidswhopoptodaywillrocktomorrow*.

If **Soma Records** had done nothing else but release the original vinyl version of Daft Punk's 'Da Funk', its reputation as arbiter of techno tastes would have been sealed. Since 1991, Soma has produced quality and quantity with releases by international techno treasures Jeff Mills and Felix Da Housecat and the prolific output of their founders, Slam. Both **Numbers** and **LuckyMe Records** have followed suit since the noughties with enviable rosters of international electronica artists, while **Scotch Bonnet Records** roots out the reggae and dub vibrations from home and away.

The city also boasts newer indie kids on the block, **Olive Grove Records** and the not-for-profit **Last Night From Glasgow**, named after the opening lines of ABBA's 'Super Trouper', with its flourishing crowdfunded catalogue of new and veteran Scottish artists. All of these small but mighty operations are run with love, vision, industry, wit and commitment. Glasgow's music scene would be diminished without them.

RECORD SHOPS

Glasgow's record shops have always been more than simply retail outlets. As places to hang out, make new friends, forge connections and form bands, the best of them have been creative hubs, intrinsic to the city's musical development.

While larger department stores, including Boots and Woolworths, often housed fondly remembered music departments, the seeds of one of the town's first independent shops were sown in 1956, when young Gloria Blint experimented with selling a few 78s in her mother Betty's dress shop on Battlefield Road. The idea proved so successful that **Gloria's Record Bar** was swiftly established, boasting a reputed stock of 100,000 records and tapes.

From the mid-80s to the late 90s there were over 130 record shops in the city. Beloved gathering places now gone but not forgotten include Listen, Casa Cassettes, Bruce's, Graffiti, 23rd Precinct, Bloggs, Virgin and Tower, to name just a few.

Another legendary boutique appeared in the early 90s, when record collector Simon Black opened a department in the Byres Road branch of booksellers **John Smith & Son**. Initially the record stacks were located beside the Children's department, meaning confusion reigned when the Children's section staff unfamiliar with either the music or Simon's particular filing system covered during his lunch break.

The shop was soon accorded its own space on the bookshop's top floor and became a mecca for buyers hunting obscure and imported

Monorail, one of the city's friendliest and most passionate record stores.

vinyl. An important addition to its staff was Stephen McRobbie of the Pastels. Authors David Keenan and Brian Hogg, DJ Andrew Symington (aka Divine), and Belle and Sebastian's Sarah Martin also did time at Smith's, while bands dropping by to play small-scale instore sets included Teenage Fanclub, the BMX Bandits and V-Twin, who got drenched when the heavens opened on their rooftop gig.

The shop closed in 2000 and is now a Starbucks. But happily for record lovers, Stephen McRobbie used the John Smith's experience to go on to co-found (with Dep Downie) Glasgow's best-loved record shop, **Monorail**, which nestles within the vegan café bar Mono in King's Court. Monorail continues to go from strength to strength, hosting a varied programme of instore gigs and events, though even their unflappable staff were surprised when US superstar Lana Del Rey, then living in Glasgow, phoned to ask if she could drop off a few copies of her new album for sale. Meanwhile, there's a chance to refresh memories of the record stores gone by at the permanent exhibition *Spinning Around – Glasgow's Remarkable Record Shops* in the city's Riverside Museum.

FESTIVAL CITY

Glasgow prides itself on its bottomless appetite for a party and its all-embracing bear hug of a welcome, making the city a natural host for all manner of music festivals, from experimental offerings Tectonics and Sonica via the small but perfectly formed Glasgow Americana Festival and indie fiestas such as the Tenement Trail and Glas Goes Pop to the hands-in-the-air clubbing jubilation of the Riverside Festival.

TRNSMT is a relative baby on the scene but also the big beast, hosting 50,000 revellers over each of its three days on Glasgow Green. The music policy is unabashedly commercial – if it's Saturday, it must be Liam Gallagher/Lewis Capaldi/Calvin Harris. In terms of contributing to the local economy, Paul Heaton did it best in 2023, standing the city a round by setting up a tab in five local boozers.

Glasgow Jazz Festival, established in 1987, is the oldest and classiest swinger in town, although these days it's a youthful, bijou affair supporting the city's thriving grassroots scene. Over the years, jazz giants Miles Davis, Ray Charles, Dizzy Gillespie and Sarah Vaughn have all played, while Tony Bennett eschewed a car service to walk the short distance from his George Square stage to his hotel, mingling with his audience as he strolled.

Celtic Connections has banished the January blues for more than thirty years, selling around 130,000 tickets per annum to folk fans from home and away with its eclectic roots roster, encompassing Sir Tom Jones, classical percussionist Dame Evelyn Glennie, Senegalese sensation Baaba Maal and the mighty eighty-strong Grit Orchestra alongside its nurturing of the next generation of players via the legendary Danny Kyle Open Stage. The Festival Club skirls long into the eventful night – following one skirmish over 'whisky and a woman', one of the antagonists dried out in police cells over the weekend, insisting he would only converse with a Gaelic speaker to secure his release.

Every August, the city hosts the World Pipe Band Championships on Glasgow Green. Since 2003, this has been the cue for the National Piping Centre to mount **Piping Live!**, a week-long fiesta of the finest bagpiping talent. Despite buying a set of R.G. Hardie bagpipes and *Highland Bagpipe Tutor* books 1 and 2 from the Centre in 2011, Bob Dylan has yet to feature.

I LOVE YOUR FRIENDS, THEY'RE ALL SO ARTY

The esteemed Glasgow School of Art has played as much a part in the development of Glasgow's music scene as any rock venue, with long-established links between the city's music and visual arts scenes.

Famous graduates include the late **John Byrne** who designed album cover artwork for artists including The New Humblebums, Stealers Wheel, Donovan, Gerry Rafferty and Billy Connolly. Byrne's exquisite hand-painted guitar for Gerry Rafferty was a highlight of the 2018 *Rip It Up* exhibition at the National Museum of Scotland. The Beatles commissioned a painting which eventually appeared as the cover of *Beatles Ballads*, signed by Byrne under the pseudonym 'Patrick'. Byrne wrote the acclaimed BBC TV series *Tutti Frutti*, following the exploits of ageing rock 'n' rollers The Majestics, with Glasgow's Art School as a location.

Leading fashion designer **Pam Hogg** cites music as her biggest influence. Her first band, Rubbish, regularly supported the Pogues. Hogg's clothes, including her signature punk-inspired catsuits, were most famously worn by Siouxsie Sioux. During the 90s, Hogg formed her own bands, Doll and Hoggdoll, supporting Blondie and the Raincoats in the early 90s.

Visual artist **Jim Lambie**, shortlisted for the Turner Prize in 1995, credits being around musicians in Glasgow as a major influence. He was a member of indie band the Boy Hairdressers with Norman Blake in pre-Teenage Fanclub times. Best known for his psychedelic floor installations, his work is immersed in pop culture. He has designed album covers for Primal Scream and Joe McAlinden/Linden and his public art includes the much-loved Album Pathway in Barrowland Park (see page 82).

Richard Wright, winner of the Turner Prize in 2009, played in the band Correcto with former Franz Ferdinand drummer, Paul Thomson. David Shrigley, another Turner Prize shortlist nominee, has designed covers for musicians including Malcolm Middleton and Belle and Sebastian.

The Transmission Gallery on King Street, set up by GSA graduates in 1983, gained a reputation for great openings and after parties. Franz Ferdinand's 'Do You Want To' summed up its appeal with the lyric, 'Here we are at the Transmission party/I love your friends, they're all so arty.'

Glasgow-born Pam Hogg forged her bold and provocative career in London's mid-80s post-punk scene, and her front-row regulars include Nick Cave, Siouxsie Sioux and Nick Rhodes. In 2014, her London Fashion Week show highlighted the plight of Pussy Riot and the struggle for gay rights in Russia.

EPILOGUE

THE FUTURE IS BRIGHT

In this book we have celebrated the local legends and international players but the next wave of talent is not waiting for permission to join the party. Instead, they are making their own scene, whether graduating from the wealth of music courses in establishments such as Riverside Music College and the mighty Royal Conservatoire or building community connections well beyond the city centre.

The Conservatoire's excellent jazz department has produced Mercury Music Prize and Scottish Album of the Year Award alumni Fergus McCreadie and corto.alto, who head up a very cool grassroots community. The homegrown hip-hop scene ranges from Govan veteran Steg G to acclaimed rappers Bemz and Eyve, from Nigeria and Zimbabwe with love, while K4CIE, Rebecca Vasmant and Supermann On Da Beat are the DJ/producers du jour.

Glasgow's love affair with noisy guitars means you are never officially more than ten metres away from a member of an upcoming indie band. Allow us to recommend Conscious Pilot, Dead Pony, Brenda and the Wife Guys of Reddit, but the list really does appear to be endless. Alice Faye, Evie Waddell and L.T. Leif are bewitching new voices and former busker Dylan John Thomas has advanced from al fresco on Argyle Street to multiple sell-out appearances at Barrowland.

Glasgow's fertile music culture was built on the traditions of generations of immigrants who settled here in the city and on a brisk transatlantic trade in folk, blues and country sounds. The city still attracts artists from all over the world to its vibrant and varied music scene. Such is the dynamic DIY nature of this creative ecosystem that, by the time you read this, there will be a whole new batch of contenders for Glasgow's greatest hits.

See you in the mosh pit.

Ballroom blitz: this mural on the side of the Barrowland Ballroom is inspired by Douglas Stuart's Booker Prize-winning novel *Shuggie Bain*.

SOURCES AND ACKNOWLEDGEMENTS

The authors and publisher would like to thank Judith Bowers, Justin Currie, Damien Love, Carla Da Luz, John Martin, Andy Prevezer, Jill Rodger, Andrew Symington, Duglas T. Stewart and Anne Ward. Special thanks to Phil Eaglesham whose enthusiasm, experience and unique guiding have endeared him to so many of Glasgow Music City Tours' guests.

Books

Nirvana: A Tour Diary, Andy Bollen, Metro Publishing, 2013.

Glasgow's Lost Theatre: The Story of the Britannia Music Hall, Judith Bowers, Birlinn Ltd, 2014.

Nileism: The Strange Course of the Blue Nile, Allan Brown, Polygon Books, 2011.

The Sydney Devine Story, Sydney Devine, Black & White Publishing, 2005.

Tenement Kid, Bobby Gillespie, White Rabbit, 2021.

Simply Thrilled: The Preposterous Story of Postcard Records, Simon Goddard, Ebury Press, 2014.

McGinn of the Calton: The Life and Works of Matt McGinn 1928–1977, Glasgow District Libraries, 1987.

The History of Scottish Rock and Pop, Brian Hogg, Guinness Publishing, 1993.

Brickwork: A Biography of The Arches, Kirstin Innes, David Bratchpiece, Salamander Street, 2021.

You Don't Have to Be in Harlem: The Story of the Most Celebrated Rock Venue in Britain, Russell Leadbetter, Mainstream Publishing, 1995.

Dear Green Sounds: Glasgow's Music Through Time and Buildings, Kate Molleson, Waverley Books, 2015.

Barrowland: A Glasgow Experience, Nuala Naughton, Mainstream Publishing, 2013.

Never Understood: The Jesus and Mary Chain, Jim Reid, William Reid et al, White Rabbit, 2024.

Walking Back Home, Ricky Ross, Headline, 2022.

One Love, One Life: Stories from the Stars, Billy Sloan, Black & White Publishing Ltd, 2023.

Under A Rock, Chris Stein, Corsair, 2024.

Whatever Happened to the C86 Kids?: An Indie Odyssey, Nige Tassell, Nine Eight Books, 2023.

Small Hours: The Long Night of John Martyn, Graeme Thomson, Omnibus Press, 2020.

Theme for Great Cities: A New History of Simple Minds, Graeme Thomson, Constable, 2022.

TV/ online links

A Taste of Divine: David Peschek: The Quietus: https://thequietus.com/interviews/divine-retrospective/

Apollo, Sold Right Out: http://www.glasgowapollo.com/

CCA: Centre for Contemporary Arts: Archive: https://www.cca-glasgow.com/archive/about-the-archive

Ella Logan, FBI Record: The Broadcast 41: https://broadcast41.uoregon.edu/biography/logan-ella

Lost Glasgow: https://www.facebook.com/lostglasgowofficial

Interview with Andi Lothian: Dundee Courier: https://www.youtube.com/watch?v=OJUk_PSgWNU

Radio Clyde Documentary: HD Warrior/ Philip Johnston https://www.hdwarrior.co.uk/2024/07/05/radio-clyde-documentary/

University of Glasgow: QMU, Queen Margaret Union: https://www.qmunion.org.uk/

University of Strathclyde: History of Student Union: https://www.strathunion.com/union/history/

When Motown Came to Britain: BBC/ Wiseowl Films

Newspapers/ Magazines

Daily Record
Glasgow Live
Glasgow Times
The Herald
The List

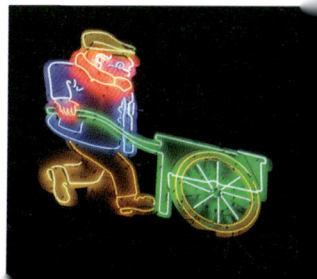

PHOTOGRAPHY CREDITS

Greetings from Glasgow mural, Sauchiehall Street, courtesy of authors
Alex Harvey, Clutha mural by Rogue-One, Art Pistol and Ejek, Gorbals
     Street, courtesy of authors
Lulu © Alamy
Jim Kerr © Alamy
Postcard record sleeves courtesy of authors
Matt McGinn and Hamish Imlach, Clutha mural by courtesy of authors
Billy Connolly mural by Rachel Maclean, Gallowgate, courtesy of
     authors
The Blue Nile courtesy of Birlinn Ltd
Belle and Sebastian badge courtesy of Anne Ward
Tigermilk album cover courtesy of authors
Pastelism courtesy of Anne Ward
Tiger Tim © Alamy
Debbie Harry at the Apollo © Alamy
ABC courtesy of authors/Sole Media
Glasgow Empire theatre programme courtesy of Damien Love
13th Note courtesy of authors
Splash One flyer courtesy of John Martin
Locarno dancers © Alamy
Ultravox © Alamy
Clare Grogan © Alamy
Strawberry Switchblade © Alamy
Jimmy Somerville © Alamy
Lena Martell courtesy of Konrad
Travis bus courtesy of authors

Paolo Nutini poster courtesy of authors

Del Amitri courtesy of Andy Prevezer PR

Biffy Clyro © Alamy

FFS poster courtesy of Alison Rae

Jesus and Mary Chain ticket courtesy of authors

BMX Bandits courtesy of Duglas T. Stewart/Harrison Reid

Ella Logan © Alamy

Ivor Cutler correspondence courtesy of Damien Love

Pavilion Theatre courtesy of authors

Tamla Motown tour © Alamy

Status Quo CD cover courtesy of Hewlett PR

Barrowland star, interior and signage courtesy of authors

Scotia Bar courtesy of authors

Britannia Variety Theatre poster, Harry Lauder and Vesta Tilley
   courtesy of Judith Bowers/Britannia Panopticon:
   www.britanniapanopticon.org

Royal Conservatoire of Scotland courtesy of authors/Jannica Honey

King Tut's exterior and staircase courtesy of authors

Sub Club exterior courtesy of authors

Glasgow Royal Concert Hall © Glasgow Life/Paul Watt Photography

Ovo Hydro courtesy of authors

The Garage courtesy of authors/Sole Media

Saint Luke's courtesy of authors

Divine poster courtesy of Anne Ward/Andrew Symington/Catrina
   Cruickshank

Nice N Sleazy cables courtesy of authors/Jannica Honey

Frederick Douglass © Alamy

Unity Creates Strength album courtesy of authors

LNFG label courtesy of Last Night from Glasgow

Monorail interior courtesy of authors

Pam Hogg © Alamy

GMCT tour courtesy of authors/Sole Media

Shuggie Bain mural, Barrowland, courtesy of authors

Barrowland man courtesy of authors

A NOTE ON THE AUTHORS

FIONA SHEPHERD is an established music journalist who has been attending gigs and writing about the music scene since 1990. She is the chief rock and pop critic for the *Scotsman*, and also writes for *Scotland on Sunday, The List* and *Uncut*.

ALISON STROAK has been a bookseller, publisher and editor. Alison managed the legendary John Smith's Bookshop on Byres Road when it was one of the favourite haunts of Glasgow's music fraternity.

JONATHAN TREW has been writing about music, culture and restaurants since the early nineties. A brief stint as a music reporter for MTV convinced him he was more useful as a keyboard jockey than in front of a camera.

Jonathan, Fiona and Alison are co-founders/directors of Glasgow Music City Tours and Edinburgh Music Tours, which offer guided music-themed walking tours that explore the rich musical history of both cities.

GLASGOW MUSIC CITY TOURS

Since 2015, Glasgow Music City Tours have been running guided walking tours and events which explore the city's music scene. Spanning rock, pop, folk and jazz, the tours are designed to appeal to hardcore music fans as well as people who simply want to experience Glasgow through a different lens.

We welcome as many Glasgow residents as we do city visitors, and we like to think our tours feature lots of entertaining stories which are new to both groups. Led by musicians, music writers and fans, our tours are packed with tales of the artists who have stayed, played and made music in Glasgow, the venues they performed in and the audiences who make every gig memorable.

www.glasgowmusiccitytours.com